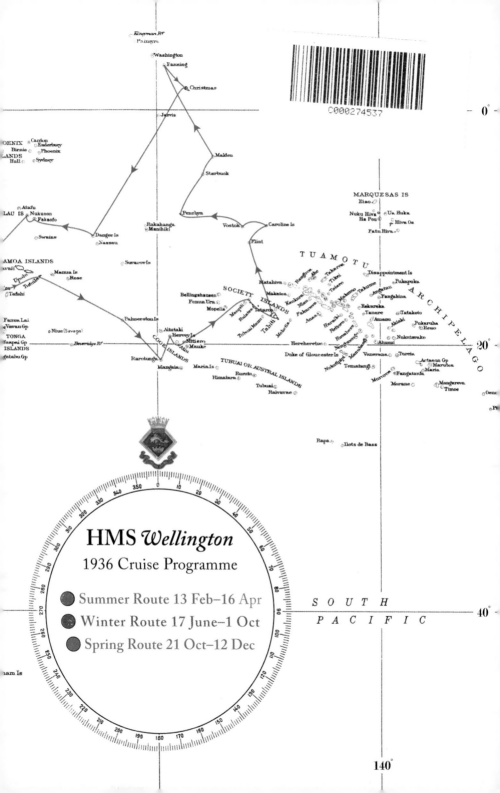

HMS *Wellington*

1936 Cruise Programme

- Summer Route 13 Feb–16 Apr
- Winter Route 17 June–1 Oct
- Spring Route 21 Oct–12 Dec

HMS/HQS WELLINGTON

HMS/HQS WELLINGTON

CAPTAIN A. D. MUNRO, FRIN, FNI

THE HONOURABLE COMPANY OF MASTER MARINERS

(MASTER 1998–99)

LONDON
THE WELLINGTON TRUST
HQS *WELLINGTON,* TEMPLE STAIRS
VICTORIA EMBANKMENT WC2 R 2PN

First Edition - 2006

ISBN 0-9553405-0-0/ISBN 978-0-9553405-0-5

Published by THE WELLINGTON TRUST,
HQS *WELLINGTON,* TEMPLE STAIRS,
VICTORIA EMBANKMENT, LONDON WC2R 2PN

© CAPTAIN A. D. MUNRO

Printed by BROWN, SON & FERGUSON, LTD.,
4–10 DARNLEY STREET, GLASGOW G41 2SD

ACKNOWLEDGEMENTS

Acknowledgement is hereby made to the many individuals, public libraries, newspapers and other sources, including Arnold Hague and his *Sloops 1926-1946,* who helped in the exhaustive research required to write this history of *Wellington*; some in this country, others scattered throughout New Zealand and Fiji, where the ship spent more than four years of her working life prior to WW2.

The greatest number of illustrations covering the pre-war period are from a collection donated to The Honourable Company of Master Mariners. These were most likely assembled by Lieut. Commander B H de Mellor, RN, who served on the ship from August 1937 to January 1940, and although neither he nor any of his relations have been successfully traced, due acknowledgement is hereby given for the most valuable contribution they make to the history of the ship while on peacetime duties in the Southwest Pacific.

For wartime records the Admiralty War History Cases held in the Public Record Office provided valuable references of *Wellington* when serving as a convoy escort, as did the Naval Historical Branch of the MOD.

The paintings of HMS *Wellington* are by the late Captain R E Baker, a former Liveryman of HCMM who donated them to the Company in 1989.

The colour pictures showing interior views of the ship as presently berthed at Temple Stairs, London were graciously contributed by Chester Boyd & Co., Ltd.

Last but not least, due recognition must be given to Messrs Brown, Son and Ferguson, Ltd., Nautical Publishers since 1832, for their valuable help in assembling this book and their generous contribution to the cost of production.

CONTENTS

Six years after registration in 1926, The Honourable Company of Master Mariners became the first Guild to be admitted to the ancient fraternity of the Livery of Guildhall after an interval of more than two centuries. Both were considerable achievements at the time, and were followed in 1949 by the provision of a ship-borne Livery Hall in the shape of the former sloop HMS *Wellington,* moored within the City boundary at Temple Stairs on Victoria Embankment.

In the years prior to World War 2, HMS *Wellington* served for four years on the New Zealand Station, visiting many ports of that country and the British administered islands of the vast South West Pacific. During the six years of war *Wellington* provided escort to 103 convoys on the eastern side of the Atlantic, rescuing many survivors from sunken ships in the process.

Throughout the years, *Wellington* has received constant maintenance and improvement, and has become a most fitting and suitable home for The Honourable Company of Master Mariners. In 2004 the ship was honoured by the grant of World Ship Trust status and in 2005 was given over to the care of The Wellington Trust for preservation and as a lasting tribute to the invaluable co-operation that exists between Britain's Royal and Merchant Navies.

This book tells her fascinating history. Profits from its sale will help The Trust continue maintaining the ship to the highest possible standards.

ix

CHAPTER 1

DESIGN, CONSTRUCTION AND PASSAGE
TO NEW ZEALAND

The term 'sloop' in the Royal Navy was first used for a type of small sailing vessel which became extinct towards the end of the 19th century, but was revived for classes of fleet-sweeping convoy (sloops) built during the First World War, and of which, by sheer coincidence, the once RNVR Drillship, HMS *President,*(ex HMS *Saxifrage*) presently berthed astern of *Wellington* now remains the sole survivor.

During the two relatively peaceful decades between the two World Wars, most of these (coal burning) minesweepers were disposed of, other than a few retained as patrol sloops on distant stations, while updated versions were being designed to replace them. The requirement which then evolved was for the dual purpose of minesweeping in wartime and overseas service on detached colonial duties in peacetime. By 1924 it was decided initially "to build two ships of 1,300 tons displacement",[1] 266 ft. overall length, 34 ft. beam and fitted for twin-screws and geared turbines to give a maximum speed of 18 knots. Endurance was specified as 5,000 miles at 10 knots to suit both foreign station service and convoy escort work. These ships were completed in March 1929 as *Bridgewater* and *Sandwich* and 'proved satisfactory in service... for the versatility of their design on a small hull'.

From these beginnings a further thirty ships were completed before the outbreak of war in September 1939 on a progressively developed design, the original two being followed by a class of five completed 1930–31; of which one was manned by the Royal Indian Navy. A further class of four followed in 1931–32, another four in 1932–33 and yet another class of eleven between 1934–36 which also comprised *Wellington*, a second unit for Indian manning and two built in the Cockatoo Dockyard in Sydney for the Royal Australian Navy. Apart from this latter pair, almost half the total including *Wellington* was built in the naval complex at Devonport Dockyard.

In respect of armament, the first thirteen ships were equipped with either one or two 4 inch high-angle guns but the *Wellington* group had two 4.7 inch low-angle and one 3 inch high-angle in addition to 3 pdr saluting guns. In the course of time high-angle A/A guns replaced the low-angle

1

versions while 22mm. Oerlikon and later still 40 mm Bofors replaced 0.5 inch machine-guns for air defence.

As the 1930s progressed it became clear that anti-submarine (A/S) and anti-aircraft capabilities would take precedence in the design of further sloops rather than minesweeping, which thereafter developed as an entirely separate class of warship. To provide for this additional armament the three ships which followed the *Wellington* group were longer by 16 ft. and the next three again by a further ten feet while the final design of the 37 ships built during the war years were almost 300 ft. in length on a beam of 38.5 ft. and displacement of 1,925 tons. For A/S work the earliest sloops carried only four depth charges, but from the *Wellington* group onwards two throwers and 40 charges were fitted, and in the war-built group four throwers and up to 110 charges. Asdic was progressively fitted in all the sloops and from 1942 onwards Radar and the ahead-throwing Hedgehog A/S weapon as each became available.

The names chosen for the first 22 British sloops were of U.K. seaside towns and cities except *Wellington*, the fourth ship of that name in the Royal Navy, which from the outset was intended to replace one of the ageing sloops on the New Zealand station, as was *Leith* which arrived there six months earlier as a stopgap until *Auckland*, which completed in November 1938 was appropriately allotted to take her place. However she was in lieu sent to the South Atlantic station based on Simonstown and never subsequently reached New Zealand, being bombed and sunk off Tobruk in June 1941.

Of the 32 sloops in service by the outbreak of hostilities, four each were serving on the South Atlantic station or in the Red Sea or Persian Gulf area. Five were based at Hong Kong, two at Trinidad for the West Indies and two at Auckland for the New Zealand station. Six were under refit in the U.K. or with the Home Command while the remainder were at Colombo, Malta and Australia. The Indian manned ships were in their own waters.

The normal peacetime complement of the sloop and certainly that of *Wellington* comprised the Commander and four other Commissioned officers in addition to the Engineer and Gunner who shared that accommodation as Warrant officers. There were 20 Petty Officers, 7 Engine-Room Artificers (ERAs), 37 Seamen, 28 Stokers and 8 Stewards/Cooks: a total of 107. Those ships on foreign stations generally carried a number of locally engaged ratings e.g. Chinese, Somali, Maltese, West African, etc., while New Zealand personnel in training for their own service (not then a separate entity) were frequently carried in lieu of RN personnel.

The space given over to officers' accommodation was not far removed from that of a warship today. The Commanding Officer was the sole occupant of the Foc'sle Deck with a forward facing day cabin fitted with kneehole table, bookcase, safe for confidential documents and a small dining table and extension able to seat four persons. Immediately aft and to port of this space was his sleeping cabin and bathroom with a pantry to starboard. Aft of this again was the W/T office to port and a 7ft. square lobby to starboard which could also double as an extra cabin. The remaining officers were berthed two decks down in single cabins on both sides of the ship aft of the engine-room, which space also provided a spare cabin in addition to the Wardroom and Ship's Office. Each cabin measured about 8 ft. square and was fitted with bedplace outboard, kneehole or writing table, bookshelf, cupboard and compactum. Aft of this accommodation was the minesweeping store with the winch for wire sweeps immediately above on the quarterdeck. The officers' bathroom and WCs were on the deck above their accommodation adjacent to the CO's spare cabin which was equipped with a settee bed, chest of drawers, writing table and compactum, and which he used when vacating his main quarters for the Resident Commissioner when visiting remote outlying islands. The 4.7 inch shell room and 3 pdr. Magazine were immediately below the Wardroom.

Also berthed on the same (Lower) deck as the officers but forward of the machinery space was that provided for six Chief Petty Officers and seven ERAs to port, while that for 14 Petty Officers were to starboard. This was on the sleeping and messing system with hammocks and tables, settees outboard and bench type seats inboard; each man with an equivalent space of 24 sq.ft. Below this accommodation were the Provision and Issue Room, Canteen Store and Cold Store.

The messing and sleeping space for all 65 ratings was on the forward section of the main (Upper) deck between the Fo'csle and Lower Decks. Along the port side were four mess tables and bench seating for 28 Stokers and beyond a W/T Door two further tables and benches on each side of the ship for 37 Seamen. On the starboard side was a 2 berth Sick Bay with ablution cabinet, bath and WC. Hammocks were stowed in one corner of the Mess and further messing for six locally embarked Seamen in another when so required. One luxury was an ice chest and 25 gallon cooled fresh water tank. Each man had the equivalent of 15 sq.ft. of space.

The canteen and crew galley were on the centre island of the Upper Deck with the Cooks and Stewards Mess outboard along the starboard alleyway, beyond which was the washplace and WCs for CPOs and POs. The equivalent port side space was occupied by the ratings' washplace and WCs (nine basins and four WCs for 37 personnel).[2]

The *Wellington* carried 44 tons of fresh water and 337 tons of oil fuel in six tanks. Steaming on a reduced consumption of 0.5 tons per hour at 10 knots gave the ship a comfortable endurance of 5,000 miles. The 4.7 inch quick firing guns were able to elevate a maximum 30° but the 3 inch high angle gun above the CO's dayroom could attain 90°. The bridge was equipped with two 10 inch signal projectors and 3 metre rangefinder while a 24 inch searchlight was fitted on a raised platform aft of the funnel. Stowed on each side of the ship abreast the funnel was a 27 ft. whaler and 16 ft. dinghy while on the starboard side aft of the whaler was a 25 ft. motor boat; this outfit in contrast to modern destroyers and frigates carrying no more than one or two RIBs in addition to inflatable liferafts.

As the fourth of her class, *Wellington* was laid down in Devonport Dockyard in September 1933, launched on 29 May 1934 by the Hon. Lady Fullerton, wife of Admiral Sir Eric Fullerton, CinC Plymouth Command, commissioned for special trials on 7 December that year and for acceptance trials and service on 22 January 1935 under the command of Commander J B E Hall, RN, while Lieut. Commander C B Alers-Hankey was appointed First Lieutenant. The ship was commissioned with a West country crew from Devonport Barracks, and inspected by Rear-Admiral Binney, Chief of Staff to Admiral Fullerton, who expressed himself very satisfied with the appearance of the ship and her personnel. Commander Hall presented the ship's wardroom with an engraving of the previous *Wellington* built in 1816. The ship sailed for New Zealand on 5 February when telegrams of welcome were exchanged between the High Commissioner in London and Commander Hall. The outward voyage proved to be a leisurely one of three and a half months but began badly when the ship ran into a NW'ly gale which followed her across the channel and through Biscay, buffeting her severely and giving everyone a severe shaking in the process. Perfect weather with calm seas then prevailed until reaching the east coast of Australia.

Four days were spent in Gibraltar berthed opposite the battle-cruiser *Renown*, which had just been in collision with *Hood*, and during a two day call at Malta with the whole Mediterranean Fleet in port, *Wellington* was visited by many officers who expressed envy and admiration at her comfortable quarters. Further calls were made at Alexandria (five days), a day each at Ismailia and Aden and six days in Colombo before reaching

Wellington as completed December 1934

World Ship Society

Arrival at Devonport Naval Base, Auckland, 20 May 1935

New Zealand Herald

Singapore on 2 April, where the coal burning minesweeper *Laburnum* from the New Zealand station had been fitted out as a training ship for the Straits Settlement RNVR, and was in fact the ship that *Wellington* was replacing in the southern hemisphere.[3]

On 7 April *Wellington* left Singapore for two day calls at Batavia (now Jakarta) and Bali, where shore excursions were organised to give the crew a much welcome respite from long spells at sea. One day was spent at Thursday island in the Torres strait before passing down inside the Great Barrier reef to reach Sydney on 2 May in time to join the celebrations for the King's Silver Jubilee. It was here that nine ratings were transferred to the cruiser *Sussex*. *Wellington* then made a four day call at her named city before berthing at the Devonport Dockyard base in Auckland harbour at 0930 on 20 May 1935, soon after firing a salute of 11 guns to the broad pennant of Commodore the Hon. E R Drummond, CinC of the New Zealand Division. Commander Hall then made an official call on the Commodore and the other Commanding officers of HM ships, stating that: 'the Dominion had the reputation of being the most popular station in the service and many other officers envied him his command'.[4] The officers and crew were soon to appreciate the validity of this statement.

CHAPTER 2

THE FIRST COMMISSION ON THE NEW ZEALAND STATION: MAY 1935–AUGUST 1937

The New Zealand station of the Royal Navy covered an oceanic area of the Western Pacific in excess of 8 million square miles, in which lay 14 major groups of islands under British Protectorate amounting to at least 534 individually inhabited islands. Four ships were required to patrol this vast area and to train the numbers of New Zealand personnel in preparation for the establishment of a separate Royal New Zealand Navy. During the first half of the 1930s the station was covered by two of the elderly D class cruisers, *Dunedin* as flagship and *Diomede,* supported by two sloops, *Leith* and now *Wellington* in lieu of *Laburnum* re-positioned to Singapore. The two cruisers and *Leith* had preceded *Wellington* into Auckland harbour by one day after gunnery exercises in the Hauraki gulf. All four warships were expected to remain at the naval base until departure on individual cruises: *Dunedin* on 5 June for 86 days, *Diomede* on 18 June for 66 days, *Leith* on 11 June for 102 days and *Wellington* on 5 July for 76 days.

Commander J B E Hall (right) & First Lieutenant i.e. Lieutenant Commander C B Allers-Hankey (left),
Auckland, 20 May 1935   *New Zealand Herald*

After eight weeks in Auckland settling down and exercising with *Leith* in the nearby Hauraki gulf, *Wellington* sailed for her first winter cruise on 15 July by heading NNW for five days to Vila, on Efate island of the New Hebrides. Whilst in this port, advice was received that a native mission teacher had been clubbed to death by a party of savages at Bushmans Bay on the northeast side of Malekula island, 120 miles farther north. Acting at the request of the District Police official at Vila, Commander Hall decided to proceed to Bushmans bay with a party of native police to capture those responsible. *Wellington* arrived off the bay soon after midnight with every light extinguished and landed the police party while several rounds of blank shot were fired from the ship. This terrified the natives, few of whom had ever seen a European and never a ship other than a trading schooner. The local Chief and seven natives were arrested without difficulty before dawn and taken aboard *Wellington* and later left at Vila to await trial.[5]

After a further call at Bushmans bay, *Wellington* continued north on a four day passage skirting the Banks and Santa Cruz groups to reach the isolated coral island of Nauru lying 30 miles south of the Equator, where the ship berthed between the moorings used by ships loading phosphate for three days. Whilst at Nauru, Commander Hall inspected a 130 strong group of local Boy Scouts, while numerous entertainments were arranged for the crew by the local populace of natives, Europeans, Chinese and other Pacific islanders. A soccer match against the workers at the phosphate fields resulted in a win for the ship of 2 – 0. From Nauru the sloop sailed ENE for two days to anchor off Betio on Tarawa atoll of the Northern Gilbert group for a four day stay. Tarawa had a population of about 9,000, and consisted of a chain of islets on two sides of a reef, each covered with coconut palms and dense undergrowth. Calls were made at Tarawa on two subsequent occasions.

Wellington then made a three day passage ESE to the remote Phoenix island, a mere 16 ft. in height with no trees or any distinctive elevation, and remained at anchor for two days, before proceeding SW to Funafuti atoll of the Ellice group for a four day stay, then two days SSW to Rotumah, north of the Fiji group, where the local Chief presented the crew with about 3 tons of oranges, lemons, limes, bananas, pawpaws and coconuts. Similar gifts were made at other small islands and at no time was there any shortage of fresh fruit ![5]

From Rotumah the sloop sailed south for two days to the busy port of Lautoka on the northwest side of Viti Levu, the largest and highest island of the Fiji group. Six days were spent there before *Wellington* sailed overnight around the west end of the island to berth in Suva, the principal port and seat of the Government of Fiji, with a population of 35,000, including 3,000 Europeans. A further six days were spent in this capital when the Fiji Times noted 'it was hoped to arrange Association Football and hockey matches with local teams'. The sloop's officers were given as 'Lieut. M E Butler-Bowdon (Navigator), Sub-Lieut. D Vincent-Jones, Surg. Lieut. R F Stenhouse with Mr. C S Lyons (Gunner) and Mr E W Cole (Warrant Engineer)'.[6]

The final leg of this cruise, which lasted almost ten weeks, was a three day trip almost due south back to Auckland, where the *Wellington* arrived on 21 September. Eleven calls had been made at eight islands, the distance covered all the way to the equator and back being 6,880 miles; 30 days were spent at sea and 39 in port. The ship's complement was now thoroughly settled into life in New Zealand and amongst the islands of the Western Pacific.

After eleven days in Auckland, the sloop sailed on 2 October for a four week circuit of North island, starting with exercises across the Bay of Plenty, sailing down the east coast and through the Cook Strait to pass 16 miles up the picturesque Queen Charlotte sound to the South island railway terminus and ferry port of Picton. During a five day stay in this little town of 2,000 inhabitants, Commander Hall visited Havelock School and presented a handsome portrait of Lord Rutherford who received his early education there.

From Picton, it was a short hop of 100 miles around Stephens island to the Tasman bay, South island port of Nelson, where *Wellington* berthed at 1700 on 10 October for a busy stay of eight days. In customary fashion the ship was visited next morning by the Mayor, Town Clerk, Chairman and Secretary of the Harbour Board, with a return visit thereafter to the Town Hall by Commander Hall and the ship's Navigator. Schoolchildren visited the ship that afternoon and public inspection was allowed on certain days thereafter. On the 14th Commander Hall set off with his wife, who was visiting Nelson while the ship was in port, on a 100 mile trip around the shores of Golden and Tasman Bay visiting four schools, which included presenting a Union Jack to Tarakohe School on behalf of the Navy League and being lunched thereafter at the Globe Hotel by the Directors of the Golden Bay Cement Company. On the 17th Commander Hall addressed Nelson Rotary Club, 'regretted being unable to remain until Trafalgar Day in a town so associated in name with that famous battle, but suggested a local holiday on that day would not be out of place'. He publicly expressed the thanks of himself, the officers and men to the people of Nelson 'for the overwhelming hospitality which... was unequalled in his experience'.[7]

Wellington left Nelson at 1400 on 18 October and circled Golden Bay to allow the school children there, a glimpse of a modern British warship, and thereafter made the 140 mile overnight passage to New Plymouth, on the western side of North island. During the nine days in this port, which is 2 miles from the city, with a population of 30,000, a party of officers made a particularly creditable climb of the nearby Mount Egmont of 8,255 ft. (2516m.) under very soft snow conditions, while pig-hunting expeditions were organised for both officers and men.

The return passage to Auckland began on 28 October with a very rough trip up the west coast of North island with heavy beam seas both before and after rounding the North cape, making conditions on board most unpleasant. On arrival in Auckland on the morning of the 21st, arrangements were made for *Wellington* to be drydocked for her first annual refit, before exercising in early December with *Leith* in the Hauraki Gulf but otherwise remaining in Auckland over the Christmas and New Year holiday period.

The first summer cruise of *Wellington* was a complete circuit of New Zealand's North and South islands which began from Auckland on 6 January 1936, calling first at the small harbour of Tauranga on the Bay of Plenty, then at Waima cove in Tokomaru bay, some 30 miles south of East Cape. The sloop then continued down the east coast to reach Wellington on the 20th for a stay of nine days. The second leg of the cruise was out through the Cook strait and around the north tip of South island to berth in the small harbour of Greymouth, situated at the mouth of the Grey river with the entrance protected by a shallow bar and twin breakwaters. It was just possible for *Wellington* to turn within the harbour on which was situated the towns of Greymouth on one side and Cobden on the other.

The next nine days were spent amongst the remarkable and spectacular Sounds on the remote SW coast of South island. There are thirteen of these Sounds contained within a coastline of 100 miles, each from 8 to 24 miles in length; the largest dividing into several arms with a breadth rarely exceeding a mile but more often half that. The Sounds are of great depth, often exceeding 100 fathoms with precipitous tree covered shores; the entire area being devoid of habitation.

Wellington's visit to the Sounds, which were first surveyed by HMS *Acheron* in 1850/51, began on the morning of 3 February when she anchored for a single hour in Bounty haven at the head of Bligh sound, then proceeded to the restricted anchorage at Harrison cove halfway up Milford sound. This was a berth used even then by cruise ships, with the stern secured to moorings or trees on shore, which allowed passengers fine views of the falls and surrounding peaks rising to over 6,000 feet and one exceeding 9,000 feet. The sloop spent three days at Harrison cove with the motor boat, one of the whalers and a dinghy in the water all the time in calm weather with temperatures of 60°F (16°C). The daily routine began at 0530 with the hands being called with 'heave-ho, heave-ho, lash up and stow' (the hammocks) while work began with scrubbing the decks at 0600 and thereafter washing paintwork, spreading awnings, holystoning decks etc., all as required to keep the sloop shipshape and everyone fully employed. At Harrison cove, parties landed each morning to follow the tourist tracks into the hills.

With the boats hoisted inboard on return of the shore parties in the evening of the 6th, *Wellington* left Harrison cove at 0515 next day and five hours later anchored in George sound, later dropping a second anchor when the wind picked up from the SE as the temperature dropped to 49°F (9°C). Although the ship's boats were waterborne in George sound there were no landing parties and next evening the sloop departed for an overnight passage first into Thompson sound, then back to sea via Gaol passage and two hours later entering Breaksea sound, then Acheron passage, then anchoring at the head of Wet Jacket arm for a couple of hours before proceeding to the head of Dusky sound where anchorage was obtained in Supper cove that evening, 9 February, but had to be shifted next day and the second anchor put to use.

The final section of The Sounds cruise began on the morning of the 11th, when the sloop cleared Dusky sound and proceeded down the coast to enter Preservation inlet three hours later, then continued to its head to find anchorage in Cascade basin that afternoon, but remained only a couple of hours, cleared again for sea and left the Inlet at 2000 for an overnight passage along the south coast of South island and through Foveaux strait to anchor next morning in Half Moon bay off the principal settlement of Oban on Stewart island. Although the population of the island was little more than 400, the ship was thrown open to visitors for three hours that afternoon, who were warmly welcomed as the first aboard for ten days.

After little more than 24 hours in port, a Westerly gale developed next morning requiring the awnings to be furled, the boats shipped and that afternoon the ship proceeded 20 miles across to the South island port of Bluff, berthing there at 1730 hours to find the Federal Company's *Northumberland* loading meat for the U.K. as the only other ship in port. Bluff is a natural harbour, the port for Invercargill and exports the produce of the pastoral and agricultural Southland district, with berths for five meat loading ships and five others for handling oils and sulphur.

Wellington berthed alongside the wharf at Bluff in the teeth of the Westerly gale and lashing rain but was welcomed in the traditional fashion with a basket of flowers 'with the compliments of the Mayor, Councillors and Citizens of Invercargill'. The local newspaper reported the customary exchange of courtesies between civic dignitaries and the Commanding Officer but noted 'the Royal Navy was in mourning for the death of King George V and could not accept any official engagements'.[8] This did not prevent the ship being open to public inspection on each afternoon whilst berthed in Bluff.

During his visit to Invercargill Town Hall, Commander Hall recalled having been on a Senior Officers' training course when word reached him of his appointment to *Wellington* and destined for the New Zealand station. 'The other officers congratulated him on his good fortune but only now he realised the truth of their words'.[8] Since coming to New Zealand the officers and crew had been overwhelmed by the receptions and entertainments provided; 'I assure you we have been looking forward... to our visit to Southland which in England is renowned as being the Scotland of New Zealand'[8] He also commented on the convenience of New Zealand berthing arrangements which allowed close liaison with British Merchant ships, so necessary if a war situation should again arise.

The morning of the 14th brought the Shaw Savill passenger ship *Mataroa* into Bluff and this event together with *Wellington* being open to the public, attracted many visitors and sightseers to the port who arrived by car and train from Invercargill. Commander Hall, the First Lieutenant and Gunner were invited up country next day to the Eglinton Valley as guests of the Mayor and the following day proceeded on a fishing trip. On the 17th Commander Hall entertained the Mayor, Town Clerk and Chairman of the Harbour Board, together with their wives, to lunch aboard and next day in the final round of activities the Commander gave a talk to Invercargill Rotary Club.

After a hectic round of six days activities in Bluff, the sloop sailed at 1100 on the 19th for Dunedin, 140 miles up the east coast, and at 0650 next day passed inside Taiaora head to enter the 13 mile Otago harbour channel. Port Chalmers was passed at 0740 and berthing was completed alongside Rattray wharf in the centre of Dunedin at 0835. The usual courtesy calls began two hours later and with eight days in this city of the most hospitable inhabitants, there hardly seems to have been time to make entries in the log; the one most significant item being a whaler pulling race against a local RNZVR team.

Departure was made from Dunedin at 0830 on 28 February and Otago harbour cleared at 1015 for the short haul of 43 miles up the coast to the small port of Oamaru; here the sloop berthed on the inside of Sumpter wharf four hours later and remained for three days. The next port of call was Akaroa harbour on the Banks peninsula, a mountainous area mainly over 2,000 feet, situated 110 miles NE of Oamaru across the Canterbury bight. Akaroa harbour extends 8 miles inland in a northerly direction; it was a landlocked anchorage with berthage at a jetty in French bay, 6 miles from the entrance. This was for a stay of seven days for a population of 600 but was the principal watering place for the inland city of Christchurch.

Wellington sailed from Akaroa on 11 March, passed around the Banks peninsula and berthed in Lyttelton, the commercial port for Christchurch 8 miles inland, that same day. It is the outlet port for the rich agricultural and pastoral area of the Canterbury plains, the outer harbour being subject to swell but the inner one with wharves and quays well protected by twin breakwaters. A further seven days were spent in Lyttelton before the sloop continued to her name port, where she berthed on 19 March for a stay of 39 days to be joined by her sister *Leith* and the flagship *Dunedin*. During this period of time the crews carried out their annual musketry training on the range at Trentham, 15 miles by rail from the capital. All three warships left Wellington on 27 April and cruised in company around the North cape to berth at the dockyard in Auckland two days later.

The New Zealand summer cruise had lasted 114 days of which 100 days were spent in port, and having been on station for almost 12 months, the officers and crew almost considered themselves of the Kiwi breed, if not South Sea islanders at heart. Preparations were made during the ensuing seven weeks in Auckland for the next cruise to the islands, which began from Auckland on 6 January 1936 with a five day northerly passage to Lautoka, where a bombardment practice was held before visiting the Fijian capital of Suva on three occasions, interspersed with a four day call at Vatia Point on the north coast of Viti Levu and a two day passage east to Vavau of the Tonga group, where *Wellington* anchored in the landlocked harbour of Neiafu.

The main purpose of this cruise was to visit the islands lying to the north and east of Fiji, i.e. of the Samoa, Cook and Society groups, several isolated atolls up to and north of the Equator before returning to Fiji via the Union and Friendly islands; the whole being planned to occupy a period of eight weeks. During the second visit to Suva, a ship's team played a friendly football match with one from the Indian Football league: the sailors led by 3 – 0 at half time but the final score was not recorded.

The initial leg of the islands round began from Suva on 21 July with a two day passage NE to Niau Fo'ou, a remote volcanic isle lying NNW of Vavau, then on to Pago Pago on Tutuila island of American Samoa for a three day stay. The route then followed a two day course of ESE for a daylight call at the remote Palmerston atoll, the most southerly of the Northern Cook group, consisting simply of six sandy islets covered with coconut palms inhabited by 90 islanders, who apparently 'spoke a strange kind of English'.[9] A schooner visited annually with supplies and collected copra.

From Palmerston atoll it was a two day leisurely cruise SE to Rarotonga, the principal volcanic island of the Lower Cook group with a population of 6,000 including 200 Europeans, one being the Resident Commissioner. Rarotonga also had a hospital and an institution maintained by the London Missionary Society. *Wellington* remained there for three days before sailing 120 miles NE to reach the very small Hervey islands, well wooded and just 60 feet high to the tops of the trees, with a mere eight inhabitants employed in collecting copra for export. This was a brief daylight call on 4 August, followed by a similar call at the larger Atiu next day, which boasted five villages and a population of 1,400 also engaged in the copra trade. From Atui in the Lower Cook group the sloop made a two day passage NE for three calls in the mountainous volcanic Society islands, five days at Bora-Bora, four days at Papeete on Tahiti and overnight on Moorea. Although the administration of these islands was French, a British consular officer was resident in Papeete and British liner services called there en route to Australia or New Zealand.

The next section of the cruise visited eleven remote and isolated islands as far north as Fanning island, 220 miles north of the equator and covered a distance of 4,530 miles. Daytime calls were made at Flint, Caroline,

Vostock, Starbuck and Malden of the Line islands, at Danger island of the Northern Cook and Fakaofo and Nukunono of the Tokelau group. Three days were spent in English harbour of Fanning island, two days in the lagoon of Christmas island (both administered as copra plantations by the Gilbert and Ellice Colony) and a single night at Penrhyn of the Northern Cook group. The sloop returned to Suva for seven days before making a two day call at Nukualofa of the Tonga group en route to Auckland which was reached on 1 October. The total steaming distance on this cruise was 9,992 miles, having spent 55 days in port and 45 at sea.

Wellington remained in Devonport dockyard for three weeks then set off for the last cruise of the year by sailing from Auckland on 21 October 1936 for a seven week trip visiting seven ports in North and South islands of New Zealand. The first two days at sea were spent exercising across the Bay of Plenty and around East cape to berth in the small port of Gisborne on the northern side of Poverty bay. This was the first place in the Dominion where Captain Cook landed, in 1769, with a monument close south of the entrance to record that historic event.

Four days were spent in Gisborne before the sloop continued with an overnight passage of 90 miles down the coast and around the Mahia peninsula to berth next morning within the breakwater harbour at Napier, under the bold white cliffs of Ahurire bluff. The town lies on the western side of Hawke bay, on a peninsula known as Scinde island and is the capital of that district. The usual courtesy visits were made on the morning of arrival, following which the ship was open for public inspection on most afternoons while entertainments were laid on for the officers and crew and included cricket, rifle shooting, golf, tennis and billiards. A cricket match against the local High School ended in a draw, Commander Hall having scored 50 runs and the Navigator one. A local band played on the wharf while the ship was open for inspection on Sunday afternoon.

On 4 November the sloop departed Napier for the relatively long haul of 345 miles to make a second visit to Lyttelton on South island, remaining there for seven days, then four days at Timaru, an artificial breakwater harbour with berths for half a dozen vessels and chief port of South Canterbury district. The sloop then proceeded northwards, through the Cook strait for a second visit to Nelson, then nine days in the capital and finally a most unusual visit to the very small port of Dargaville on the west coast of North island and situated 40 miles up the Wairoa river. The entrance across a constantly shifting bar was negotiated with some difficulty, while the shallow river with numerous shifting banks posed additional problems. The sloop remained three days at Dargaville but never returned there. The final passage of the year was made around North cape to berth in Auckland on 12 December where the sloop remained for six weeks and exchanged some ratings while Commander G N Loriston-Clarke replaced Commander Hall and Commissioned Engineer V D Hodge was appointed in lieu of Mr Cole. The Commodore of the NZ Division inspected the ship on 18 December.

The first two cruises of the year were conveniently short to provide an opportunity for settling down amongst new surroundings. The sloop left Auckland on 23 January 1937 for the 38 mile passage across Hauraki Gulf to the small anchorage off Coromandel town within the bay of that name, being the first warship to make an official visit there for one hundred years. On the 27th in the absence of a Minister of the Crown, Commander Loriston-Clarke, who was accompanied by his officers and a detachment of seamen who made an efficient guard of honour, laid the foundation stone of the new county chambers in Coromandel. This was the Commander's first public engagement which proved to be a most colourful occasion and 'very fitting for Coromandel's history that a naval officer should perform such an act'.[10] The Commander was then presented with an inscribed silver trowel by the Chairman of the County Council. The sloop returned to Auckland that same day and remained in harbour for a period of seven weeks.

The second cruise was of four weeks duration, leaving Auckland on 15 March for exercises en route to a brief call in the capital city, Wellington, then four days at Akaroa and two further calls in her name port before proceeding to the Hauraki gulf to exercise with *Leith* and the Leander class cruiser *Achilles*, the latter having arrived on station six months earlier in relief of *Diomede* and from January 1937 carried the Flag of Rear Admiral, New Zealand Division, in lieu of *Dunedin* which then returned to Chatham.

On 4 May 1937, *Wellington* left Auckland for a third cruise to the South Sea islands, which began with a five day passage north to Suva to remain in port there for thirteen days and represented the Crown during the Coronation ceremonies for King George VI on the 12th. This included the firing of a Royal Salute and Commander Loriston-Clarke with a party of officers and men took part in the parade through the city.

The sloop left Suva on 22 May with a party of scientists who had arrived by the passenger liner *Niagara* from Auckland, and were then taken on a four day passage NE to land on Canton island, 150 miles south of the

Equator, to observe an eclipse of the sun at the beginning of June. Shore parties were landed to assist the scientists and concerts were held to help pass the time. Some notice boards calling attention to Great Britain's possession of the island were nailed to the boles of coconut trees (it later came to be jointly administered by the US and Great Britain). Canton Island was an important refuelling stop on several trans-Pacific air routes and a station was maintained there for the submarine telegraph cable. *Wellington* anchored within the lagoon close to the settlement, inhabited then by Gilbertese islanders, and after thirteen days returned south and landed the scientists at Apia harbour, the capital of Western Samoa.

The call at Apia was of two days, whence the sloop again turned north to make brief daytime calls at the three atolls of the Tokelau islands which lie between the Phoenix and Samoa groups, i.e. Fakaofo, Atafu and Nukunono. *Wellington* then returned to Apia, made a four day stop at Pago Pago, back again to Apia and then set off on a three day passage eastward for a one day visit to the uninhabited Suvorov atoll of the Northern Cook group where she anchored for the night inside the lagoon. The cruise then continued ESE for four days at Moorea and six at Papeete on Tahiti, (both visited eleven months earlier), thence SW for one day at Rarotonga of the Lower Cook, then a short overnight passage to the most northerly of that group, Aitutaki, where *Wellington* anchored for the night on the western side. This island rises to a peak of 450 feet, has a population of about 2,000 and a Resident Agent. Aitutaki was first discovered by Lieutenant Bligh, of HMS *Bounty*, a few days before the mutiny in 1789.

From Aitutaki the sloop proceeded on a SW course directly to Auckland where she arrived on 31 July, having speeded up latterly to allow a Petty Officer to be hospitalised, after developing an eye infection while in the Cook islands. The entire cruise was recorded as particularly uneventful with the weather generally good,[11] and occupied a period of 88 days making 15 calls in seven groups of islands, with 49 days in port and 39 at sea. Soon after arrival in Auckland *Wellington* was drydocked in the Calliope dock for annual refit and bottom cleaning and painting, the latter two tasks being undertaken by the crew.

CHAPTER 3

THE SECOND COMMISSION IN NEW ZEALAND: AUGUST 1937–AUGUST 1939

On completion of refit, *Wellington* left Auckland on 20 August for her name port, arriving there three days later to pay off the original officers and crew, with the exception of the Commissioned Engineer and Commander Loriston-Clarke, and re-commission with a new crew due to arrive from the U.K. on a scheduled sailing of the NZS passenger liner *Rangitane* on the 25th, whose outward voyage was marked by the customary though unscheduled call at Pitcairn, where many took the opportunity to land and view the ship's bell of HMS *Bounty*.

Ship's Bell of *HMS Bounty* on Pitcairn island

The re-commissioning for further service on the New Zealand station took place in Wellington on 26 August 1937 under the same Commander, but with Lt. Commander B H de Mellor as First Lieutenant, Lieutenants D Vincent Jones and N G Wilmott, Surgeon Lieutenant R Vaughan Jones, Mr V D Hodge, Commissioned Engineer and Mr. R Motts as Gunner.

The rough landing place. Bounty bay on Pitcairn

"Evening Post" Photo

A naval draft arrived yesterday by the Rangitane under the command of Lieutenant-Commander B. H. de C. Mellor (left) and Lieutenant N. C. Willmott. A portion of the draft is seen at the rail of the Rangitane as the vessel berthed.

New Zealand newspaper coverage of the arrival of the Second Draft at Wellington aboard the NZS liner *Rangitane*, August 1937. Inset are First Lieutenant in charge of the Draft, Lieutenant Commander B H de C Mellor and the Ship's Navigator Lieutenant N C Willmott

New Zealand Herald

PITCAIRN
SPRING MEETING

HELD ON

RANGITANE RACECOURSE
MONDAY, 16th AUGUST 1937

BY KIND PERMISSION OF
CAPTAIN A. W. McKELLAR, R.D., R.N.R.

PROGRAMME.

COMMENCE 8.45 P.M.

JUDGE:
Mr. C. MUNDELL

DICE THROWER:
Mrs. JENKINS

STARTER:
Mr. D. CAMPBELL

CLERK OF THE COURSE:
Mr. GLOVER

VETINARY SURGEON:
Mr. A. FITZHARDINGE

STEWARDS:
Mr. N. BENNETT   Lt. Com. MELLOR

TOTE STEWARDS:
U. ROOKIM   I. PINCHIM

Second draft en-route to join in New Zealand. Race Card of liner *Rangitane* when at Pitcairn, August 1937. First Lieutenant Mellor acting as Steward

Minesweeping exercises with HMS *Leith* and RNZVR personnel,
September 1937

Wellington believed anchored off Coromandel, September 1937

In accordance with Admiralty policy the previously classified Imperial Patrol Sloops were now re-styled as Escort Vessels and were to prove their worth in the dark days that lay ahead.

On 30 August the sloop left Wellington on a shakedown coastal trip to the Hauraki gulf, arriving there three days later for eight days of intense exercises and drills, returning then to Auckland to find the cruisers *Achilles* and *Leander* in port, the latter having arrived a few weeks earlier in relief of and with the Chatham crew from *Dunedin*. The New Zealand Division was then made up of two each modern cruisers and escort vessels. Also in Auckland at this time was the training and depotship *Philomel* and survey ship *Endeavour*.

After a brief four days in Auckland the sloop sailed again on 14 September for a second visit to Coromandel, then moved north for a four day call at Port Fitzroy, a small anchorage inlet on the west side of Great Barrier island, on the NE side of Hauraki gulf. *Wellington* then moved up the coast to visit three inlets on the remote NE coast, beginning with five days at Mangonui situated 40 miles SE of North cape. After the usual visit by the Port officials, the Captain went ashore in civvies to a Maori dance of welcome.

The Captain in civvies watches a Maori dance of welcome at
Mangonui, September 1937

The Maori welcome dance at Mangonui

The Ship's Rugby team which played against Kaitaia County while at Mangonui, September 1937

There was a dinner and official welcome followed by a Naval Ball that first evening in port; next morning, school children visited the ship, there was a soccer match at Kaitaia that afternoon and an Earthquake Ball that evening. The third day in port was marked by a visit to 90 mile beach and lunch at Awanui and on the last day a ship's team played rugby against Kaitaia County but the score is unknown.

The next call was four days at Whangaroa wharf where the Captain was taken on a motor trip to the Forest of the giant Kauri trees. School children visited next morning with the public in the afternoon, and on the third day a rugby match was played against Kaio Club. The last call of the cruise was one of six days at Russell wharf in the Bay of Islands; the sloop returned to Auckland on 8 October for a stay of almost three weeks.

The 1937 spring cruise of *Wellington* was virtually a repeat of that in 1935. Departure was made from Auckland on 26 October going direct to Picton for a seven day visit where the ship was open to visitors on two afternoons; cricket matches were played against both a local side and a team from Marlborough College, the ship scoring a creditable 308 runs in two innings against 107 of the local side. A ship's Concert Party gave a performance in the Navy League Hall and also at Remwick, 20 miles up country. Much of the enthusiasm and support of the sports and social activities of the ship's company emanated from the First Lieutenant and the Navigator, which latter post also carried the title of Sports Officer.

Wellington berthed at Picton, South island, October 1937, with the Union Company's overnight Wellington ferry *Tamahine*

The Picton call was followed by six days at Nelson where the vessel arrived at 1900 hours on 5 November. Next morning the customary courtesy calls were made by the Mayor and Town Clerk and by the Chairman, Secretary and Harbour Master of the Harbour Board. Return calls were then made by Commander Loriston-Clarke and Lieut. D Vincent-Jones. The vessel departed Nelson at 0630 on the 11th for a ten day visit to New Plymouth, where a cricket match was played against the local High School, pig hunting parties were laid on in addition to tennis, golf and bowling. The Harbour Master's staff gave the ship a whaleboat race, trout fishing was available and the Navy League took parties of officers to Mount Egmont. The officers and crew gave a concert at the State Theatre which raised £34 for Charities including the Ship's own fund.

There was a swimming carnival, the Commander and one officer had lunch at the Rotary Club and on the Sunday afternoon, when the ship was open to the public, the Taranaki Regimental and Pipe Bands played on the wharf. The sloop returned to Auckland on 25 November, to remain there over Christmas and the New Year preparing for the next islands cruise. A cricket match against the cruiser *Achilles* on 22 December resulted in a win for the *Wellington* with an innings of 104 against 71 from the cruiser.

The vessel next left Auckland on 4 January 1938 to make an unexpected cruise of 2,240 miles to Canton island, last visited in May 1937. The main purpose of the visit was to exchange radio operators at the shore station, who resided in Fiji, and was made at the request of the High Commissioner for the Western Pacific, Sir Arthur Richards. *Wellington* left Suva on the 13th with the relief operator, Mr T H Manning and two officials making the round trip. During the four day passage north, a NW'ly gale was experienced, blowing severe at times and lasted two days but no damage occurred.

Wellington anchored in Canton island lagoon on the morning of the 17th, landed Mr Manning and embarked Mr F H Rostier. The only other European on the island, Mr G V Langdale, acting administrative officer, volunteered to remain for a further term. "Also landed were a quantity of coconuts for planting and it was noticed that some of those planted last year were showing signs of sprouting. About 17 months supply of stores were also landed and the two shore tanks filled with 800 gallons of fresh water".[(12)] After a few hours at anchor the vessel left for Hull island distant 105 miles to the south.

The Ship's Officers, January 1938, Back row L to R:— Mr V D Hodge (Commsd Engineer),
Surg.Lieut R Vaughan Jones, Sub Lieut Crawley, Mr R Motts, (Gunner). Front row L to R:—
Lieut.Cmdr B H de C Mellor, Commander G N Loriston-Clarke, Lieut N G Wilmott (Navigator/Pilot)

The Ship's Chief and Petty Officers, January 1938

The Ship's Company, Auckland, January 1938

The Flagpole at remote Canton, the first island to be jointly administered by Great Britain and the
United States (Stars and Stripes in background)

The mission to Hull island, where *Wellington* anchored off the reef, was to land stores for the only European resident, Captain Jones, who lived there with a number of Gilbertese who had recently settled there producing copra. The vessel remained only a few hours, returned to Suva on the 24th and was back in Auckland on the last day in January.

Mr Jones, Manager and sole European on Hull island

Notice placed on Hull island by HMS *Leith*, 1936

It was whilst in dock at this time that excessive shaft bearing wear was reported, similar to that found on *Leith* which required replacement of the bearings in Sydney. The *Wellington* spent ten days in Calliope dock and completed refit alongside the dockyard then sailed on 9 March for a three week stay in Wellington, to allow the ratings' attendance at the Trentham musketry course.

From the capital city the ship moved to Akaroa for five days minesweeping exercises with *Leith,* during which time RNZVR ratings from South island were embarked and then returned via Wellington to Auckland on 14 April. A week later both vessels were at sea for two days divisional gunnery practice with the cruisers *Achilles* and *Leander* in the Hauraki gulf. *Leith* and *Wellington* left Auckland on 27 April to sail in company to Sydney, where they were placed into the hands of the dockyard on Cockatoo island six days later. During the time in Sydney, teams from *Wellington* played six Soccer matches and won 3, won and lost one each Rugby matches and drew at two Hockey matches.

Replacement of the worn shaft bearings in Sydney occupied a period of six weeks, following which both vessels sailed direct on their respective planned winter cruises to the Southwest Pacific islands, *Leith* to carry the Queen of Tonga on Royal visits to outlying islands.

Wellington left Sydney on her fourth winter cruise on 13 June 1938, proceeding NE for seven days to arrive at Suva 0630 on the 20th for an overnight stay, thereafter continuing to Hull island also for an overnight stay. The task here was to erect a W/T mast and to blast a hole in the reef to allow ships' boats to enter the lagoon for landing supplies. Arrival was timed for 0500 when the tide would allow the first boat carrying Mr Motts and the demolition party, the First Lieutenant with the mast party together with drums of cement, explosives, supports and stays for the mast, to land on the open coral shore. Even so each man had to be carried across the jagged coral by natives to reach the shore. Subsequent boat trips brought the breakfasts and limejuice ashore, followed by the stores intended for Mr Jones, the Manager and sole European on the island which was otherwise worked by natives from the Gilbert and Ellice group preparing copra for export. All of the work was completed and *Wellington* sailed again 24 hours later.

The next call was a brief one at Canton island, which has a landing stage and anchorage inside the lagoon and where it was hoped to establish a commercial flying-boat base. Both Britain and the U.S. had W/T shacks there and jointly administered the island which had been visited by *Wellington* 12 months earlier (q.v.) when a party of Stokers built a brick pillar upon which the Shipwrights painted a large Union Jack.

From Canton it was a four day trip NE and across the Equator to Washington island. This was another half-day visit where stores were lowered overside by accommodation ladder davits into native boats,

Stores being landed via native boats at
Washington island, June 1938

as the swell made it impossible for ships' boats to land on the beach.
A small coastal ship was lying off awaiting the swell to subside for
loading copra.

The next call was at Fanning island, 75 miles to the SE, where the sloop
remained for two days. Anchorage was obtained close to the landing stage
which served the cable station as the halfway link between Vancouver
and Suva, and notable for being shelled by the German cruiser *Emden* in
WW1. It was observed that Mr Farquharson the W/T operator had a better
residence and was better found than the Resident Commissioner!

The wife of the Resident Commissioner and W/T Operator, Mr Farquharson,
in the Commissioner's residence at Fanning island, July 1938

The sloop invited the whole island of 19 people to a concert held on the
after end of the Boat Deck, with various sketches including 'Albert and the
Lion' while music was supplied by six mouth organs and a drum. These
were the days when ships' crews made their own amusements and were
doubtless the better for it.

The First and Surgeon Lieutenants rehearse on the Quarterdeck for a concert, July 1938

The next leg of the cruise was an overnight trip SE to Christmas island for a further two day stay, the island being discovered by Captain Cook on the *Resolution* on Christmas Day 1777.

Wellington anchored off Christmas island, July 1938

It is another copra island, about the size of the Isle of Wight, and was let to a Frenchman with a Czech manager who had no pay for three years. The islanders were Tahitians who lived in two settlements named London and Paris. The Commander was taken for a drive by the Manager in a rather ancient car. Twelve fowls carried on the Quarterdeck from Suva were landed here and during the two weeks on board were officially believed to have produced but a single egg!

The settlement known as 'Paris' on Christmas island, July 1938

Commander Loriston-Clarke and Manager with his ancient car on
Christmas island, July 1938

The First Lieutenant, the Manager and Captain at
Christmas island, July 1938

From Christmas island there was a further two day trip SSE to Malden island, where the sloop remained a mere six hours but sufficient for a difficult landing in very heavy surf to find the once guano producing island to be worked out and deserted, although good surf boats remained stored in a shed. The sloop had previously visited in 1936 and erected wooden piles with a plaque to record this and was suitably updated. The final call on this first leg of the cruise was at Starbuck island, also at one time worked for guano, but also judged to be uninhabited although a landing could not be made because of the very heavy surf. The sloop then made a leisurely eight day passage back to Suva, arriving early morning on 17 July for a nine day stay.

The Manager and notice on Malden island proclaiming visits by *Wellington*
in August 1936 and July 1938

Although the time in Suva provided a rest from the ceaseless round of visiting remote atolls, there was also much scraping and painting to be done, the exercise of fire and repair parties, refitting whalers and the skiffs sailing gear, etc. The ship was berthed alongside *Leith* and prompted a soccer match which *Wellington* won 3-2 thus qualifying to meet *Achilles* in the final. Whilst in port, *Wellington* gave a concert in Suva Town Hall, playing to an almost packed house in aid of the Cottage Home and Naval charities. This was attended by the Governor Sir Arthur and Lady Richards, prior to both sloops witnessing their departure next day on the New Zealand liner *Niagara*. The *Wellington* also played 6-a-side soccer, 10 minutes each way, between eight sections of the ship's company, i.e. Officers, P/Os, Forepart, Afterpart, CPOs, Stokers, etc.

The second part of the islands cruise began with a three day stay at the sugar exporting port of Lautoka on the NW side of the main Fiji island. Parties were taken from the ship to a village Kava ceremony in which the root of a tree is pounded and watered to make an intoxicating drink tasting like aspirin. The sloop then proceeded NW on a three day passage to the remote Tikopia island, a densely wooded British protectorate lying to the

The Union SS Co's liner *Niagara* leaves Suva with the retiring Governor, Sir Arthur and Lady Richards, July 1938. Viewed from *Wellington* with *Leith* alongside

A typically perfect Fijian house

Native boys on Tikopia island salute visitors from HMS *Wellington*, August 1938

New Zealand Herald

Native canoes welcome *Wellington* to Tikopia island, August 1938

NE of the New Hebrides. The ship obtained a good berth in Ringdove anchorage on the western side of the island where a boat landed with some officers and crew to make their number with friendly villagers who were found to be Polynesians living in circular huts. In January 2003 the then 1,800 islanders survived a cyclone which devastated their crops, trees and water supplies by hiding in mountain caves.[13]

Bushmen invited aboard *Wellington* at Tikopia island, August 1938, the first visit by an
HM Ship since 1892

The ship left Tikopia next morning to proceed NW for a same day call at the Santa Cruz islands, situated between the Solomons and the New Hebrides, and from there it was a three day trip NNE to Ocean island, 53 miles south of the Equator which like its sister Nauru, exports large quantities of phosphate but has no harbour. *Wellington* was secured between mooring buoys normally used to accommodate the loading phosphate ships and remained rather uncomfortably for three days, sailing again on 8 August to make a three day call at Butaritari and six days at Tarawa, both of the Northern Gilbert group. This was followed by daytime visits to Nonouti, Beru and Tamana of the Southern Gilberts, a further daytime call at Nanomea and four days at Funafuti, both of the Ellice island group. From this latter atoll the vessel proceeded 280 miles SSW to the isolated Rotumah island lying to the northwest of Fiji, first discovered by Captain Edwards of HMS *Pandora* when searching for the *Bounty* mutineers in 1791. An overnight stop was made at Rotumah where the officers and 40 sailors landed to watch a dance in the forenoon, followed by a talk, a football match

The British Residency on Ocean island, August 1938

The British Resident comes aboard at Ocean island, August 1938

Village Meeting place on Butaritari, August 1938

Officers and villagers at Nanomea island, August 1938

and lunch with the natives. *Wellington* then returned via Lautoka to reach Auckland on 9 September. The cruise had occupied 88 days over a distance of 10,360 miles with the time in port equalling that spent at sea. There were 21 port calls made in six separate groups of islands.

During the seven week period that *Wellington* remained in Auckland, the armed forces in the U.K. were mobilised for war but again stood down with the signing of the 'Peace in our time' 1938 Munich agreement of 25 September. *Wellington* was then preparing for a five week cruise to the North and South islands of New Zealand.

Returning to Auckland in dirty weather, September 1938

The spring cruise of 1938 was the only one which *Wellington* made in a clockwise direction around South island, and having left Auckland on 25 October, proceeded first to Gisborne on the east coast of North island to make a six day visit as a repeat of that two years earlier. The next call was a similar repetition with ten days in Lyttelton, whence she departed on 14 November to pass around the tip of South island and entered the west coast Sounds to cruise that area for five days, which included locating a comfortable anchorage in Broughton arm of Breaksea sound, before continuing up the west coast into Cook strait and Queen Charlotte sound for a single night in Picton. The final leg continued up the west coast and around North cape to reach Auckland on 28 November.

The customary lay-over period of six weeks including Christmas and New Year was in 1938/39 extended to eleven weeks. This was by far the longest inactive period since the ship was first commissioned four years earlier and was never subsequently surpassed for over five years of almost continuous service under arduous wartime conditions.

"These sloops .. are maintained principally for police duties etc in the South Sea Islands" *(Official Extract)*

Inside of Ship's Christmas Card 1938

"These sloops... are maintained principally for police duties etc in the South Seas Islands"   (Official Extract)

Wellington anchored in Broughton arm, Breaksea sound, November 1938

Climbing/Hillwalking party from the ship in the west coast Sounds,
November 1938

Wellington in Broughton arm, Breaksea sound, November 1938

Lieut.Cmdr Mellor at the final Sydney cocktail party, March 1939

Wellington departing Sydney 31 March 1939

On 7 January 1939 Commander R E Hyde-Smith relieved Commander Loriston-Clarke as Commanding Officer, and on 13 February the ship left Auckland for a six day visit to Port Fitzroy, followed by five days at Russell, and thereafter crossed the Tasman Sea to arrive in Sydney on the 24th for a further refit at Cockatoo island, presumably to check the shaft bearings fitted there nine months earlier. Once again the ship was accompanied by *Leith* and on completion of refit while based on Sydney, both ships gained valuable anti-submarine experience, together with ships of the Australian squadron, when exercised with the British submarine *Phoenix* on a visit from Hong Kong. The five weeks in Sydney were long remembered for the parties, even the Sydney Morning Herald commenting that 'the lads of HMS *Wellington* and *Leith* are giving the local lasses a marvellous time… parties, just about every night during the week… small informal ones and dinners. They were entertaining again last night, I believe… 'while a later report said 'at Susan Phillips cocktail party there was a momentous meeting between Lieut. Willmott of the submarine *Phoenix* and Lieut. Willmott of *Wellington* who had never met before, but told amused guests they had been getting each other bills for years!' The vessel returned to Auckland on 6 April and thereafter spent a week on gunnery practice with *Leith* in the Hauraki gulf, and a further week of sea training with a detachment of local RNZVR officers.

Rehearsal for gunnery inspection, May 1939

The winter island cruise of 1939 was scheduled to cover New Caledonia, the New Hebrides, Solomon islands, Gilbert and Ellice group, Fiji, Eastern Samoa, the Society and Friendly islands throughout a period of almost 20 weeks but had to be curtailed due to the threatening situation in Europe. It was about this time that *Leith* and *Wellington* were considered to be units of the Royal New Zealand Navy, rather than the NZ Division of the Royal Navy, but were not destined to remain with it for long.

On 15 May *Wellington* sailed for RNZVR minesweeping training in the Hauraki gulf and a full rehearsal for the Commodore's inspection with Divisions on the Upper Deck before returning to Auckland on the 17th. After six weeks based in Auckland, which included a week in Calliope drydock for painting ship, HMNZS *Wellington* sailed for the South Pacific islands on 18 May 1939, starting with a rough four day trip to Suva, where she arrived at 0700 on the 22nd for a four day visit.

It was here that the sloop embarked His Excellency the High Commissioner of the Western Pacific, Sir Harry Leslie, KCMG, together with his ADC for the western section of the cruise, which began with a three day trip SW to Noumea in French New Caledonia. During a very full two day visit, the Commissioner visited the Chief de Cabinet, was presented to government officials, held a conference and dined at Government House.

Ship's officers with His Excellency the High Commissioner for the Western Pacific, who embarked at Suva in May 1939 for a ten week cruise of the islands.
Centre row L to R: Lt Cmdr Mellor, His Excellency Sir Harry Leslie, Commander Hyde-Smith, Lieut. Wilmott

Next day there was a ceremony at the Monument aux Morts, an island excursion, a cocktail party aboard *Wellington* and a further dinner at Government House. The last morning was spent visiting nickel blast furnaces before H.E. re-embarked on *Wellington* to sail at noon on the 29th for the New Hebrides.

Wellington berthing at Noumea,
27 May 1939

Noumea awaits the landing of His Excellency,
27 May 1939

Guard of Honour for H.E. landing at Noumea, May 1939

H.E. goes ashore at Noumea, May 1939

During the next ten days, six calls were made in the British and French jointly administered New Hebrides group of islands, beginning with three days at the port of Vila on Efate island. The sloop anchored in the harbour at 0900 on 31 May, fired a salute of 11 guns to the French Resident Commissioner followed by the same for his British counterpart. Representatives of each party visited the ship that morning, while His Excellency and ADC landed in the afternoon for return courtesy calls and inspection of a native gathering.

H.E. landing by canoe at Mele island (Vila), May 1939

Dinner was laid on at the British Residency that evening and during the next three days, H.E. held conferences at Vila, was driven to a lagoon, visited the French hospital, had tea at the Tennis Club, cocktails at the British Residency and dined at the French Residency while a small dinner was given aboard *Wellington* for six British and French Judges. All of the ship/shore work was handled by the ship's own motor boat.

The next call was one of 24 hours at the small volcanic island of Pau Uma where the ship was met by the Presbyterian Mission Minister who organised a programme for H.E. to study native life and mission work. The Minister dined aboard the ship with his wife. The sloop then made the 40 mile passage to Bushmans bay on Malekula island, where H.E. received on board local British residents and later went ashore to look over the British Agency building and plantation.

The sloop then crossed to Baldwin cove on the south side of Espiritu Santo and anchored close to Venui islet, where the British Agent boarded to pay his respects to H.E., who then landed to inspect the Presbyterian Mission Teacher Training Institute, and met some of the locals, reported to be cannibals.

Reported as cannibals at Baldwin cove (New Hebrides),
June 1939

The Superintendent and his wife dined aboard *Wellington* that evening. Next morning, H.E. and party landed to inspect the Agency and meet local Residents, together with some local natives and bushmen, the latter being shy of warships. H.E. then re-embarked and the sloop sailed up the Segond channel to anchor off the French Agency at Luganville bay, whose representative boarded to pay his respects. H.E. and party then landed to visit the agency, hospital and school. Next day there was a visit to the Adventist Mission, whose Superintendent and wife were invited aboard for lunch. Aperitif d'adieu was held aboard that evening and *Wellington* crossed next morning to Lolowai bay on Oba island where the Bishop and Archdeacon of Melanesia came aboard. H.E. and party then landed and were entertained by the Mission staff. Both churchmen and their wives dined aboard the sloop that evening and next morning, 10 June, *Wellington* departed the New Hebrides for a two day trip NW for three calls in the Solomon Islands.

This proved to be the one and only visit of the sloop to the British Solomon Islands Protectorate, a chain of islands extending in a WNW direction for 600 miles.

The Pilot book of the time warned that the 'treacherous nature of the natives has been modified, but every precaution should be taken against surprise by small parties dealing with them.

The population of the Solomons was 450 Europeans, 200 Chinese and 93,350 Melanesians and Polynesians. The climate was not healthy on account of the humidity, and all Europeans staying any length of time got Malaria before long'.[16] Wounds and sores in that climate were liable to change into malignant ulcers.

Wellington arrived in Port Mary on the western side of Santa Ana island in the forenoon of 12 June, to be confronted by half a dozen large canoes each manned by 20 warriors, the outermost one carrying a flag to mark the outer edge of the reef. The ship was then surrounded and followed into the anchorage.

Wellington arrives at Santa Ana, Solomon Islands,
June 1939

In the short space of that day H.E. and party together with some of the ship's complement went ashore by canoe to watch three separate dances staged especially for the visitors: a war dance of the warriors, a dance by the fairer sex and that of the tree men, derived from the belief that man originated there.

H.E. Party & Ship's Officers watch a dance at Santa Ana,
June 1939

The Dance at Santa Ana to welcome H.E. and Party,
June 1939

The sloop then proceeded to Aola bay on the NE side of Guadalcanal for another 24 hour stay and where there were several villages, a coconut plantation and a Government station. The island is of volcanic formation, densely wooded with mountains rising to over 8,000 feet, but with peaceable Melanesian natives. From Aola bay the ship made the 35 mile passage through Sealark channel and Iron Bottom sound to berth alongside Government wharf in Tulagi harbour, where the Resident British Commissioner of the Solomons was stationed.

Wellington alongside at Tulagi, Solomon Islands, June 1939

This was a six day call with the customary dinners and cocktail parties but also much golf, tennis, cricket, swimming, billiards and football matches with sides from the ship to provide some relief from shipboard routine. The ship then crossed Indispensible strait for the 65 mile passage to Auki harbour on the south side of Malaita where anchorage was found for the next two days. Here a war dance and shark dance was given by bushmen, while a ship's side played cricket with the natives and were put out for 14 runs. So far as is known, Auki was the last call of a British warship in the Solomons; the Japanese began to occupy the islands in January 1942 and were not completely expelled (by US and New Zealand forces) until March 1944.

The Cricket Team returns to the ship at Auki, Solomon Islands, June 1939

Wellington left the Solomons on 23 June and sailed 640 miles NE for a three day stay at Nauru, then moved 160 miles east for a six day stay at Ocean island, although this was visited ten months earlier. At both these islands the H.E. party carried out the usual round of calls at the Residencies, toured the phosphate workings, held receptions and visited various points of interest.

The next leg of the cruise was 300 miles ENE to Tarawa atoll of the Northern Gilbert group for a similar six day visit as in August of the previous year. Tarawa was followed by an overnight call at Abemama of the

H.E. inspects the local Constabulary, Tarawa atoll, Northern Gilbert islands, July 1939

HMS *Wellington* anchored off a South Pacific island pre 1939

Water-colour by Captain R E Baker

The Ship's badge borne by HMS *Wellington*
1935–1947 being the armorial bearings of the
City of Wellington, capital of New Zealand, with
the motto *Suprema ut Olim* (Supreme as Ever)

HMS *Wellington* as a Western Approaches escort in 1942

Presents for H.E. at Vaitapu, Ellice islands,
July 1939

The Navigator/Pilot inspects a necklace at Vaitapu, Ellice islands,
July 1939

same group, and a further overnight at Vaitapu, where the Commissioner landed by canoe and was carried up the beach *in situ*, to be confronted by gifts of yams, chickens, eggs and a whole pig. This party included the Government Land Agent, the First Lieutenant and Doctor and all made a visit to Vaitapu College for Natives.

The last two calls in the Ellice group were at Nukufetu, which also involved a canoe landing and proved to be a very happy and friendly island where 3 tons of gifts including pigs, chickens, eggs, coconuts, yams and sweet potatoes were heaped upon the visitors. Four days were spent at Funafuti where the local Governor requested *Wellington* to stage a concert. This was held on board complete with new songs and sketches and proved to be not only the best to date but also the very last; the sloop being en route to her war station seven weeks later. On 30 July Funafuti was left behind on the overnight passage 260 miles SW to Rotumah.

Wellington's immaculate motor boat was worked hard in the islands

An elaborate ceremony had been arranged in Rotumah for the opening of a new Roman Catholic school built by the local population which was officially opened by H.E, after the customary speeches. The school was then inspected and a series of dances given by the children and teams from neighbouring villages. The next event was a ceremony in which a rare root, normally taboo, was pounded to a paste and served to the distinguished guests, tasting rather like caramel cream. This was followed by a sumptuous lunch accompanied by liberal quantities of red and white wine.

Both Tarawa and Abemama were occupied by the Japanese in December 1941, the former being converted into a considerable fortress to protect an airstrip from which their bombers were able to attack similar US bases on the Ellice islands, particularly at Funafuti, 700 miles to the South. Tarawa and Abemama were recaptured by US Marines in November 1943.

From Rotumah, *Wellington* returned to Suva where she arrived on 25 July for fourteen days of relative civilisation after almost ten weeks of continuous island visits and lonely ocean passages. The High Commissioner and ADC now disembarked and gave a dinner at Government House for all the ship's officers, while 'tennis, golf, soccer, rugby, hockey, rifle shooting, swimming, yachting and boxing were laid on for all the ship's company. Dances were held nearly every evening and for several of these the sailors were admitted free',[14] and in addition, the local sugar refining company, 'provided outings to Nukulau and refreshments for 200 men'[14] when the cruisers *Leander* or *Achilles* were in port.[14] Even while *Wellington* lay in Suva, *Achilles* arrived from Auckland on 3 August and remained in port until the 9th. During the islands cruise, soccer teams from the sloop had won 7 out of 10 games.

From Suva the sloop made a four day visit to Levuka on the east side of Ovalu, a small island on the east side of the main Fiji island, which like Suva provided an alongside berth, and was shared with the passenger liner *Maunganui* on a cruise from New Zealand. From Levuka the sloop began the eastern section of the cruise with calls planned for Pago Pago, Penrhyn, Vostock, Caroline, Flint, Bora Bora, Papeete (Tahiti), Moorea, Rarotonga, Palmerston atoll, Vavau and back via Suva to reach Auckland on 7 October. The initial call of five days at Pago Pago on Tutuila island of eastern Samoa took place as planned, berthing alongside the U.S. Naval Station jetty and from where *Wellington* departed on the morning of 19 August on the four day passage ENE to Penrhyn island. Two days later a signal was received ordering a return to Auckland 'with despatch', then distant 1920 miles, and so the sloop put about to steer SW but continued at her normal cruising speed of 9 knots.

Wellington shares the berth at Levuka (Fiji) with the Union Company's passenger liner *Maunganui* on a cruise from New Zealand

Wellington berthed in the dockyard at Auckland on 30 August from her final cruise on the New Zealand station. Of the 26 escort sloops then serving overseas, fifteen were now ordered home to serve as convoy escorts, including *Leith* and *Wellington* which first proceeded to the East Indies. The last winter cruise to the Pacific islands had lasted 104 days with a single call in New Caledonia, three on Fiji, six in the New Hebrides, three in the Solomons, two in the phosphate islands, two in the Gilberts, three in the Ellice group plus Rotumah and Pago Pago. The ship was now prepared for war service and remained in Auckland for a mere five days.

CHAPTER 4

THE RETURN FROM NEW ZEALAND TO THE U.K.

With a departure from Auckland on 3 September, a matter of hours before Britain declared war on Nazi Germany, it must have been obvious to all on board that *Wellington* was unlikely to return to New Zealand in the immediate future. Proceeding not at the customary cruise speed of 10 but rather 13 knots, *Wellington* took her departure from the 15 mile light on North cape of New Zealand's North island that night, steering then for the Breaksea Spit, 200 miles north of Brisbane at the southern entrance to the inside route through the Great Barrier reef. The ship refuelled at the Queensland port of Townsville on the 9th, continued through the Torres strait and Timor sea to pass through the Roti strait into the Savu sea, thence by Sumba and Lombok straits, around Bali and into the Java sea and so by Carimata strait to reach Singapore on the 19th.

For the next six weeks *Wellington* and *Leith* were based on Penang and Singapore patrolling the Malacca straits, until ordered home. *Wellington* left Penang on 2 November, refuelled and stored at Colombo on the 9th and Aden on the 17th where she was ordered to Freetown for escort duties. The Suez Canal was transited on the 23rd with departure from Port Said next day but on passage through the Mediterranean the ship had to put into Malta for eight days boiler repairs. Sailing again on 5 December and refuelling at Gibraltar on the 9th, *Wellington* reached the steamy heat of Freetown on the 16th.

Freetown had been established as a homeward convoy assembly port with the first departure on 14 September. *Wellington* sailed on 18 December for the U.K. as escort to a convoy of only ten ships, followed next day by *Egret*, a relatively new sloop also diverted from Singapore, escorting an even smaller though faster convoy of seven ships. *Leith* followed a week later with the next convoy of sixteen ships and was the last of the homeward sloops to pass through Freetown at this time. Four other sloops came home with Gibraltar convoys and all fifteen of those redirected from foreign stations were in U.K. ports refitting by mid February 1940.

The homeward passage of convoy SL 14, escorted only by *Wellington* and the AMC *Carnarvon Castle*, was without incident until the morning of 3 January 1940 and some 300 miles west of Ushant, when the sloop attacked a submarine contact but with unknown result, and was then ordered to detach from the convoy and proceed to Devonport where she arrived two days later, after an absence of one month short of five years. With a brief call of two days the sloop then sailed for a refit in Cardiff, boarding the suspect Belgian trawler *Guido Gezell* en route and reaching the South Wales port on the 9th. It was here that Lieut. Commander Mellor left the ship, 'the happiest he had every sailed in'[(17)], but many of the ratings remained and served on *Wellington* for the rest of her active life.

Christmas Card received by *Wellington* December 1939, from the Queen and King George VI

CHAPTER 5

WESTERN APPROACHES ESCORT
BASED ON DEVONPORT

Port time in Cardiff was limited to 19 days but undoubtedly allowed leave parties, while the ship was urgently prepared for war service by landing the saluting guns and minesweeping gear, which were then replaced by depth charge rails and throwers on the quarterdeck. Stores and ammunition were then embarked, following which Commander Hyde-Smith proceeded with the sloop in a SW'ly gale to Devonport to join the Western Approaches 1st Escort Division, first at Portsmouth, then on 8 February re-ordered to Portland for work up, but next day was sent out to meet the homeward convoy HX 18 of 43 ships from Halifax. On the 12th the Admiralty instructed *Wellington* and sister sloop *Rochester* to meet the Halifax convoy at daylight next morning in a position 300 miles west of the Scillies, however this order was almost immediately amended when both sloops were sent to search for survivors from the independent Swedish *Nidarholm*, torpedoed and broken in half that same morning. All 25 crew were certainly picked up but not by *Wellington*. Both sloops met the convoy as directed and next day reported it was dividing into two portions; that for the English Channel presumably escorted by *Wellington,* which berthed in Devonport on the 16th for ten days of repairs to her Asdic. It later transpired that *Nidarholm* had been torpedoed by *U 26*, which in turn was sunk by *Rochester* five months later.

Sailing from Devonport on 26 February, *Wellington* acted as escort to a convoy of 38 ships which formed up next day to the SW of Lands End bound for Gibraltar, and arrived there without incident on 4 March, spent 16 days in that port and returned with a homeward convoy of 36 ships from which she later detached to return to Devonport on the 29th. Three days later she sailed again to escort a small outward convoy of six ships bound down channel until to the SW of Lands End when she returned to Devonport on 3 April. After a further three days in port, *Wellington* joined another Gibraltar convoy this time of 49 ships which formed to the SW of Lands End and reached the Rock free of incident on the 16th. Thirteen days were spent there from where she returned with a homeward convoy of 25 ships until detached on 6 May, and returned to Devonport next day for six days to make good defects and the fitting of a DG coil.

On 10 May the so called 'phoney war' on the Western front of Europe came to an end as the Germans opened their major offensive against the waiting Allied armies. *Wellington* left Devonport on the 13th to patrol the Dover straits where so much traffic was crossing to and from France and after refuelling in Dover, left there on the 19th as escort to an outward convoy of eleven ships which left Southend that morning, and detached from it two days later to return to Devonport and complete the earlier defects.

The sloop again left Devonport on 26 May to meet an outward convoy of 40 ships for Gibraltar which formed up to the SW of Lands End two days later. Detachment from this convoy was made prior to arrival Gibraltar when *Wellington* transferred to a homeward convoy of 24 ships, which proceeded to Liverpool after detaching the sloop to the west of the channel on being ordered to Dover, which was reached on 2 June.

The major evacuation of the BEF from Dunkirk was by then almost complete with 338,226 British and French forces successfully brought across the channel. On 9 June *Wellington* left Dover with the Canadian destroyer *Restigouche* to rendezvous with the elderly destroyer *Saladin* off Cap de la Heve, for Operation Cycle: the evacuation of troops from nearby Le Havre. By next morning however, it became known that 51st Highland Division, which was attached to French forces and acting under their orders, was virtually trapped at St. Valery 30 miles NE of Havre. *Wellington* and the new corvette *Gardenia* were then directed to the beaches at Veulette at the mouth of the river Durdent and then with other small vessels to the harbour at St. Valery-en-Caux 5 miles further east. At both these places, the motor boat and whalers were used to evacuate personnel from the beaches. The plan was to evacuate the maximum number on the night of the 12th, but fog intervened to prevent all rescue ships reaching the coast and by morning the French ordered a surrender and so caused the entire 51st Division to be captured. *Wellington* returned to Devonport on the 15th.

With the Germans now occupying the coast of Europe from Norway to France, it became necessary to close the South coast ports in favour of those on the west, and so *Wellington* left Devonport for a further absence of five years on 20 June to join another Gibraltar convoy to the SW of Lands End, this time comprising 28 ships, and later detached ahead of it to reach that port on the 26th. Just two days were spent there, the sloop returning with 12 ships to Liverpool on 7 July and there joined the Western Approaches Sloop Division; this despite the 1937 Admiralty directive which re-named the class as Escort Vessels.

CHAPTER 6

WESTERN APPROACHES ESCORT
BASED ON LIVERPOOL

In common with many other sloops and escorts, *Wellington* was based in the Gladstone Dock in Liverpool for the next twelve months. Outward and inward convoys were now routed through the North Channel and north of Ireland, the first by this means for Gibraltar sailing from the Bar Light Vessel with *Wellington* as escort on 17 July 1940. This was a convoy of 20 ships which arrived safely nine days later, the sloop departing with a homeward version next day of 24 ships carrying evacuees for the U.K. On 9 August the destroyer *Westcott* joined *Wellington* as escort to this convoy which was then 240 miles west of the Irish coast; two days later when 60 miles WNW of Tory Island, the Admiralty ordered an emergency alteration to north for reasons unstated, but was probably due to the presence of a U-Boat which torpedoed and sank the AMC *Transylvania* on the previous morning exactly on the track of the convoy. No attack developed and all ships reached Liverpool safely a day behind the sloop on the 13th.

Wellington next sailed from Liverpool on the 19th with a Gibraltar convoy of 30 ships and returned with another of 21 ships to Liverpool on 19 September, while the destroyer *Garland* joined as additional escort on the homeward leg.

It was at this period of the war until April 1941 that Atlantic convoys were only given A/S escort as far as 19° West (effectively 200 to 300 miles west of Ireland), due to the chronic shortage of escorts and further exacerbated by the fruitless employment of many flotilla vessels scouring the seas as hunting groups in search of U-Boats. *Wellington* next left Liverpool on 27 September with the corvette *Gladiolus* as escort to such a convoy of 32 ships which was due to disperse three days later. In the evening of the 29th the Admiralty advised the convoy was being shadowed by a U-Boat, and although no attack developed, ordered the escorts to remain with the convoy and postponed dispersal for a further day. At 0345 on 1 October, the lookouts on *Wellington* spotted smoke on the horizon which on investigation was found to be the burning Royal Mail liner *Highland Patriot*, homeward bound from the Plate, which had then been torpedoed and set on fire. The sloop picked up 169 survivors from the ship's boats, including the Master, and thereafter continued an Asdic sweep ahead of the convoy until dark, when it was dispersed. *Wellington* then proceeded at maximum speed for the Clyde and landed the survivors at Gourock on the 4th, before returning to Liverpool two days later.

The sloop next left Liverpool on 11 October as escort to a Gibraltar convoy of 36 ships and arrived there just ahead of it on the 23rd, where Commander I H Bockett-Pugh, DSO RN assumed command in lieu of Hyde-Smith who had held the post for almost 22 months. After eight days in harbour, the sloop left again with a convoy of 51 ships for Liverpool, assisted by the destroyer *Inglefield*, and it was during this passage when approaching the latitude of Finisterre, that a Halifax convoy in mid Atlantic was attacked by the German *Admiral Scheer*, which sank the escorting AMC *Jervis Bay* and caused the convoy to scatter. The Admiralty considered the *Scheer* might then make for Brest and so ordered *Wellington* and the convoy from Gibraltar to reverse course and return to that port. Two days later the sloop was in collision with the small British tramp *Sarastone*, and on 11 November the convoy was amalgamated with one from Freetown to make a combined formation of 75 ships. An Admiralty report then stated the convoy had been sighted by enemy aircraft and on the 15th a Focke-Wulf Condor attacked and bombed the Elder Dempster passenger ship *Apapa*, which soon was ablaze and had to be abandoned. *Wellington* reached Liverpool with the remainder of the convoy on the 18th.

A further outward convoy of 44 ships was escorted from Liverpool with the destroyers *Vansittart* and *Veteran* on 30 November, until dispersal on 4 December, following which a homeward slow convoy of 32 ships from Sydney (Cape Breton) was met on the 5th and escorted into Liverpool two days later, where *Wellington* remained for 11 days with five of them spent in drydock from the 13th for bottom cleaning and painting.

The last task of 1940 was with part of a troop convoy bound for the Middle East. *Wellington* cleared the Bar Light Vessel at 1600 on 18 December with the Liverpool section of the convoy, comprising the Shaw Savill *Tamaroa* (carrying the Commodore), PSNC *Orduna*, Ellerman *City of London*, Booth's *Anselm* and Belgian *Elisabethville*, together with five storeships and a Mine Carrier. The Clyde section of five troopships and six storeships was joined with in the North Channel next morning, following which the convoy proceeded out to the westward. Andrew Weir's *Ernebank* broke down for a short while on the forenoon of the 21st, rejoined later but broke down again at 1600 and was left behind with defective steering gear and two destroyers standing by.

At daybreak on the 22nd *Wellington* was detached to stand by *Ernebank* which was then ordered back to the Clyde from a position 50 miles west of Tory Island. Next day the sloop was ordered to detach from *Ernebank* (which subsequently arrived safely in the Clyde), and proceed SW to meet a homeward Freetown convoy of ten ships. In the afternoon of the 26th, *Wellington* encountered a small Hungarian steamer hove-to, but later met the convoy being escorted by the destroyers *Highlander* and *Harvester*. When 80 miles west of Inishtrahull on the 29th, this convoy was attacked by German aircraft which bombed and set on fire the Hain *Trevarrack*, which had to be abandoned in a sinking condition but was re-boarded next day and towed into Rothesay Bay three days later. This ship was again bombed while under repair in Glasgow but returned to service only to be torpedoed and sunk with the loss of all 44 persons on board in June 1941. *Wellington* arrived in Liverpool with the Freetown convoy on the last day of 1940.

The first escort trip of 1941 proved to a be a brief one of nine days, sailing from Liverpool on 10 January with 28 ships which were dispersed to the westward four days later, following which the sloop met an inward convoy next day of 21 ships from Sydney (CB), later detaching from it in the North Channel and returning to Liverpool on the 19th. After seven days in port repairing defects, *Wellington* proceeded northabout to Rosyth for two days de-storing and then continued to Dundee where she arrived on 1st February for a much needed refit, the first since leaving Cardiff twelve months earlier.

The refit in Dundee lasted almost seven weeks, during which time it is believed Type 286 Radar was first fitted. The sloop left on 19 March, called in at Rothesay on the 21st and berthed in Liverpool next day to resume service with Western Approaches Command. Two days later the sloop departed with a convoy of 31 ships from which she detached on the 29th before its dispersal in 19° West, following which she proceeded north to a position 170 miles south of Reykjavik where she joined a homeward convoy of 30 ships from Halifax. This formation had been attacked a few hours earlier by *U 48* which sank four ships in less than two hours. This U-Boat was to become the most sucessful in terms of tonnage and ships sunk and was withdrawn for training duties in June 1941.

Wellington arrived in Liverpool with the Halifax convoy on 3 April to be re-deployed back to the Gibraltar route and was assigned only three days in port, during which time the Commanding Officer was replaced by Lieut. Commander WFR Segrave DSC, who remained for the next 19 months until October 1942.

Departing Liverpool with an outward Gibraltar convoy of 47 ships on 6 April, this passage occupied 15 days and was completed without incident or enemy interference. Whilst en route, *Wellington* received orders to replace a sister sloop *Aberdeen* for the next homeward convoy sailing from Gibraltar on the 24th. This allowed a brief three days in port, the return passage with 15 ships was also incident free, the convoy arriving in Liverpool on 12 May while *Wellington* detached in the North Channel and proceeded into the Clyde for 11 days of boiler cleaning and general maintenance.

The sloop sailed with the Clyde portion of the next Gibraltar convoy on 26 May, joined with the Liverpool section in the North Channel to make a formation of 39 ships and reached their destination on 7 June, but not without loss. These convoys made a wide diversion passing about 150 miles SW of Cape St. Vincent to avoid interference from the long range Focke-Wulf aircraft based at Bordeaux-Merignac. On this occasion an Italian submarine was at the diversion point which attacked the convoy on the morning of the 6th and sank two ships; one being Swedish which lost 15 of her crew of 21. The other ship was Hogarth's *Baron Lovat* from which *Wellington* picked up the Master and all 34 crew and gunners. Six hours later enemy aircraft attacked and sank the British *Glen Head* with the loss of 27 of her crew of 36. The return passage began from Gibraltar on 14 June with a convoy of 14 ships and with the escort strengthened by the submarine *Olympus*. On the day after departure and south of St. Vincent the convoy was attacked by two Focke-Wulf Condors but no hits were obtained. On the same day the Admiralty warned that the convoy had probably been reported by U-Boat but no attack developed and all ships and escort reached Liverpool safely on the 29th.

By the end of June 1941 a further five sloops were in service, plus 155 corvettes and the first two conversions of destroyers into long range escorts. Also in June there arrived on loan, ten of the US Coastguard Cutters, which taken together, allowed a re-allocation of Britain's steadily increasing escort forces. Beginning in mid July, the Freetown convoys were to be given escort throughout rather than at the start and end of their passages, the 15 available sloops and the ten US Cutters were to be used on this route and based on Londonderry. Corvettes from Freetown would escort the convoys between that base and about latitude 19° North, where the long-range sloops and cutters would take over while the reverse would occur on the outward passage with the long-range escorts fuelling at Bathurst in The Gambia.

Wellington made what proved to be her last departure from Liverpool for four years on 14 July 1941, escorting 40 ships for Freetown with the ex US Cutters *Culver* and *Landguard*, renamed from British Coastguard stations. There was no interference with this convoy, the sloop taking 150 tons of fuel overnight on 24/25 July at Ponta Delgada in the Azores; an arrangement for escorts which had only recently been concluded with the Portuguese Ambassador in London. Both the convoy and *Wellington* reached Freetown on 1 August, having detached *Culver* and *Landguard* into Bathurst to refuel.

The return passage from Freetown began on 8 August with a convoy of 18 ships, the two cutters joining from Bathurst next day and proceeded without incident to reach Liverpool on the 28th, while *Wellington* detached in the North Channel with a section for Oban and then moved to Londonderry, berthing alongside the oiler late on the 27th and moving upriver next morning to secure alongside *Culver* at the quayside in the city. The sloop now transferred to the 'Derry Sloop Division and with intent to be in harbour over the next two weeks, leave parties were despatched to Devonport.

CHAPTER 7

THE LONDONDERRY SLOOP DIVISION

On the morning of 12 September the sloop returned downriver to fuel again from the elderly converted *Empire Dolphin*, (operated by Gow Harrison for the Ministry of War Transport) and next morning sailed at 0850 for exercises proceeding as far west as Inishtrahull, then joining convoy OS 6 of 29 ships under escort of the sloop *Stork* and Town class ex US destroyers *Campbeltown* and *St Albans*. It was the practice then to steer from the south tip of Islay to the NW for 250 miles to distance convoys from the long-range German aircraft stationed at Bordeaux, then to pass north of the Rockall Bank before turning to the SW then South towards the Azores. The destroyer *Westcott* joined on the first night at sea to make an A/S escort of five but this only lasted until midday on the 17th when all three destroyers reached the limit of their endurance and detached to return to base or to meet an inward convoy.

By the morning of the 15th the convoy was on a SW heading with a Catalina air escort in sight for most of that day. Shortly after noon, *Westcott* reported a periscope which caused the convoy Commodore to order an emergency turn of four points (45°) to starboard but as no attack developed the usual course was soon resumed. The convoy was then 60 miles west of Rockall and that evening fog patches developed which later reduced the general visibility to one mile but had improved by daylight on the 16th. The estimated position at noon then placed the convoy 450 miles west of Inishtrahull with a falling barometer and the wind freshening from the SSW force 4 to 5. Course was adjusted to keep the wind and rising seas ahead; overnight the wind continued to increase and by 0400 on the 17th was SSW 6 and at 0800 SSE force 7. Most of the convoy were struggling to maintain headway while star sights showed only 115 miles had been made good in the past 24 hours.

Throughout the 17th the wind continued generally S'ly 6 to 7 and with the destroyers detached, the convoy was now under escort of *Stork* and *Wellington* and steering a course in the general direction of the Azores, distant 900 miles. In addition to the customary navigational entries of position, course, speed and weather, *Wellington*'s log while on convoy escort duties showed that Action Stations were exercised each dawn and dusk, gunnery circuits tested each evening, the signal book checked daily at 1200, A/S sweeps at dusk and the times at which the ordered cruising station were taken up ahead or astern or on the beam of the convoy. The violent pitching and rolling motion of these relatively lightweight sloops in the weather conditions then prevailing is not difficult to imagine.

During the 18th the wind remained at force 6 but gradually backed to the SE. The gyro compass on *Wellington* broke down for 14 hours and at 1030 the sloop was directed to search astern for a straggler, the ex Tunisian but Strick managed steamer *Brika* which was back in position by midday. Sun sights that day showed the convoy had covered 233 miles in the past 49 hours to give an average speed of 4.76 knots. Three ships were detached that evening to proceed independently for the River Plate.

By the morning of the 19th the wind had eased to force 4 and continued to back throughout that day to become ESE by the evening, with a consequent increase in the average speed to 5.6 knots. The DG coil on *Wellington* had to be switched off that morning due to a cable fire in the forward part of the ship. The new sloop *Jumna*, bound around the Cape to join the Royal Indian Navy, was met and joined the convoy escort in the early afternoon. Next day the wind continued to ease off and by late evening had reduced to light airs, allowing the convoy speed to increase to 6.9 knots and by the 21st, when 300 miles NNE of the Azores, to 7.6 knots. Course was then adjusted to pass to the eastward of these islands, the eastern extremity of San Miguel being passed at a distance of 120 miles at 0800 on the 22nd. Course was then set to pass inside and between the Cape Verde islands and headland of that name in Vichy French Senegal.

There were no incidents of note on the passage to Cape Verde which was passed at a distance of 75 miles at midday on the 30th, and by which time additional A/S escorts had joined from Freetown. At 2300 that same day *Wellington* detached for Bathurst and arrived there for a seven day stay at 0900 on 1 October. The convoy continued to Freetown and arrived there safely at midday on the 3rd after a passage of 21 days from Liverpool.

The return passage of *Wellington* from Bathurst was also made with *Stork*, escorting convoy SL 89 of 23 ships, which sailed from Freetown on 5 October. *Wellington* left Bathurst on the 8th and joined up later that day. Nothing of note occurred for the first four days until Lieut. Commander Segrave received a surprise signal from the CinCWA, commending the steaming performance of the sloop during the past three months, i.e. since transferring to the Freetown route and by which time she had spent 60 days at sea and 30 in port (which was in stark contrast to the pre-war service on the New Zealand station where only a quarter of the time was spent at sea.).

On 18 October *Wellington* signalled the Admiralty requesting confirmation that the convoy would be met with a destroyer escort, prompted by a report of U-Boats operating ahead in the track of the convoy. Two days later *U 84*, outbound from Lorient for the North Atlantic, sighted the convoy and made an unsuccessful attack soon after midnight. On the 21st a U-Boat was found on the surface by an escorting aircraft, but dived when attacked and was not further located. These events brought another outbound, *U 82*, to the scene which found the convoy that same evening, attacked at 2000 hours and sank Ellerman's *Serbino* and Hain's *Treverbyn* within the space of half an hour and with the loss of 14 crew from the former and all 48 of those on the Hain steamer. These attacks had occurred when the convoy was 340 miles west of Valentia and crossing the track of U-Boats based on the Biscay ports of France.

Three months later the sloop *Rochester* depth charged and sank *U 82* NE of the Azores from which there were no survivors. The convoy continued without further incident to reach Liverpool on the 26th, while *Wellington* detached into 'Derry to refuel then continued to Belfast for repairs and maintenance lasting 23 days.

The sloop next left Belfast on 17 November, refuelled from the oiler in Lough Foyle and joined the outward convoy OS 12 of 55 ships for Freetown. There were no incidents until the 29th when the convoy was attacked 120 miles north of the Azores by *U 43*, which torpedoed Andrew Weir's *Thornliebank* loaded with military stores and munitions for the Middle East. In the process of sinking the ship blew up with the loss of all 75 crew and gunners, but also caused some damage to the U-Boat although it survived until sunk by a US escort carrier in July 1943. *Wellington* berthed at Ponta Delgada at 0815 next morning with the escort cutter *Gorleston* and having shipped stores and 150 tons of fuel, sailed again in company at 1845 to rejoin OS 12 but had some difficulty in locating it. Both escorts detached into Bathurst on 9 December to refuel and await the next northbound convoy.

The return passage began on 14 December, *Wellington* joining the homeward SL 95 of 22 ships from Freetown next day and this convoy reached Liverpool without loss on the last day of 1941. The sloop however, was detailed to stand by the Cunard *Bothnia* for five days during this passage due to engine trouble, and did not reach 'Derry until 2 January 1942, from which much needed leave parties were organised as the time in harbour was expected to extend into two weeks.

The present Court Room configured as a dining room

Chester Boyd & Co., Ltd.

The lower staircase leading to the Court Room

Chester Boyd & Co., Ltd.

EXAMPLE CONVOYS MAP

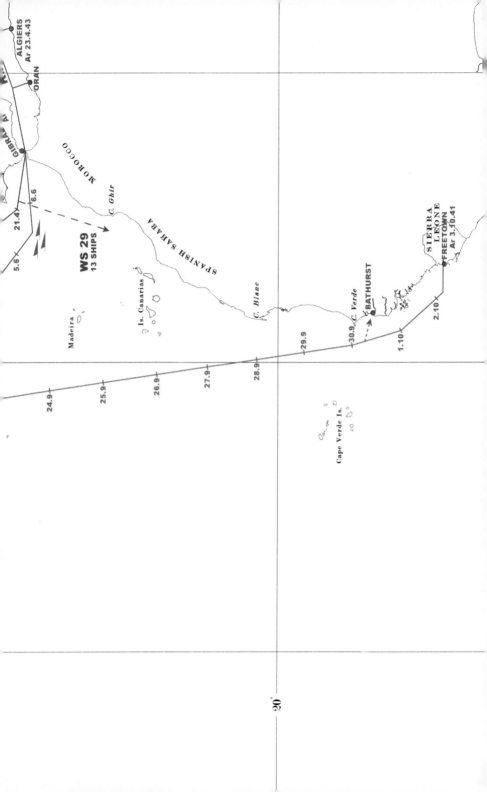

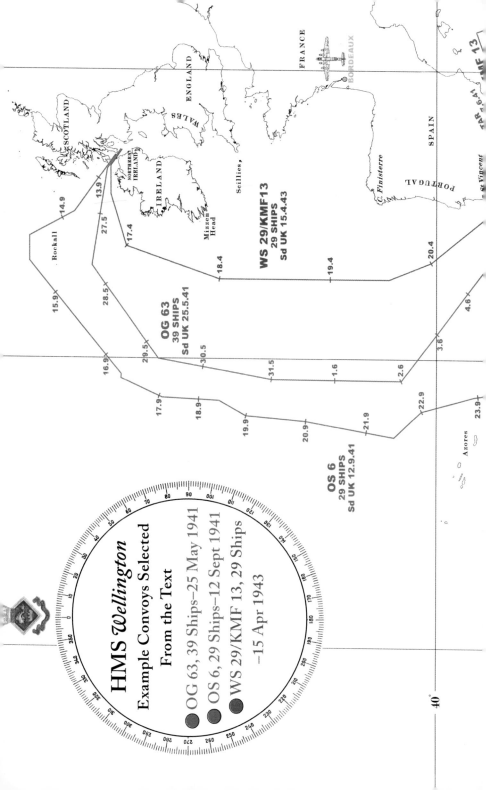

HMS *Wellington*
Example Convoys Selected
From the Text

OG 63, 39 Ships–25 May 1941
OS 6, 29 Ships–12 Sept 1941
WS 29/KMF 13, 29 Ships
–15 Apr 1943

OG 63
39 SHIPS
Sd UK 25.5.41

OS 6
29 SHIPS
Sd UK 12.9.41

WS 29/KMF13
29 SHIPS
Sd UK 15.4.43

SCOTLAND
ENGLAND
WALES
NORTHERN IRELAND
IRELAND
FRANCE
BORDEAUX
SPAIN
PORTUGAL
C. Finisterre
St Vincent
Azores
Rockall
Mizzen Head
Scillies

40°

14.9
13.9
27.5
17.4
18.4
15.9
28.5
16.9
29.5
30.5
31.5
1.6
2.6
3.6
4.6
20.4
19.4
23.9
22.9
21.9
20.9
19.9
18.9
17.9
KMF 13

Court Room configured in theatre style

Chester Boyd & Co., Ltd.

Upper staircase and Model Room

Chester Boyd & Co., Ltd.

The sloop eventually left 'Derry on 19 January 1942 and next day joined the sister sloop *Weston* as escort to a further convoy for Freetown of 42 ships. There were no incidents on passage and both sloops detached on 5 February when relieved by local escorts from Freetown to the NE of the Cape Verde islands; both arrived at Bathurst next day.

It would be hard to imagine a less salubrious place for a restful escort base than Bathurst, situated 26 miles from the Fairway Buoy and set on a promontory within the 2 mile wide entrance to the Gambia river. The sloops secured rather uncomfortably alongside the T-headed Admiralty jetty with moorings to buoys ahead and astern, this berth being situated within the small marine dockyard at the southern end of the town in a district named Half Die, and must have been the source of much ribald humour amongst the escort crews. In respect of facilities there was little to choose between Bathurst and Freetown, the former with a population one fifth the latter but distinctly unhealthy due to the proximity of marshes on both sides of the river, which wound inland through intensive jungle and villages for upwards of 100 miles.

Wellington and *Weston* returned to sea on 11 February to join SL 100 of 32 ships from Freetown which reached Liverpool without loss on 4 March. On 19 February five fast ships detached ahead with the sloop *Ibis*, a rather new escort completed six months earlier and also based in 'Derry. *Wellington* detached from the main convoy on 27 February, berthed in 'Derry that same day and moved round to Belfast on 2 March for the annual refit and docking,

Wellington **on completion of Belfast refit, April 1942**

Alongside the oiler Empire Dolphin *in Lough Foyle, after refit at Belfast, April 1942*

lasting almost eight weeks and during which time the more modern Type 291 Radar was fitted in lieu of the 286. Additional 20mm guns were also added at this time.

The sloop completed at Belfast on 26 April, fuelled in Lough Foyle and proceeded first to the Clyde then returned to 'Derry for 17 days work up before resuming service as an escort when sailing on 13 May to join OS 28 of 37 ships bound to Freetown. When to the ESE of the Azores on the 20th, this convoy was attacked by the maiden cruise of *U 159*, which sank the Elder Dempster *New Brunswick* and damaged the RFA *Montenol* and another ship. The RFA which was on a ballast passage to take station in Freetown, was at first taken in tow but was found to be impractical and had to be sunk by gunfire. Both the convoy and *Wellington* reached Freetown on the 30th where the sloop reported a leaking fuel tank requiring docking on return to 'Derry.

The return passage began from Freetown on 4 June with *Weston* and a convoy of 54 ships; *Wellington* now assigned to 42nd Escort Group and carrying 36 boxes of bullion. There were no incidents or losses to this convoy which reached Liverpool on the 23rd while the sloop detached into 'Derry the previous day and was docked for repairs to the leaking fuel tank. HF/DF may also have been fitted at this time.

After all but three weeks in 'Derry, *Wellington* sailed again amidst muted Loyalist celebrations on 12 July to join convoy OS 34 of 35 ships for Freetown. There were no incidents until daybreak on the 19th, when the convoy was 230 miles north of the Azores and found itself under attack by two U-Boats.

It transpired that *U 108* when outbound for the Caribbean had sighted the convoy on the 18th, called up three other U-Boats which came up later that day and attacked next morning. Only *U 564* was successful by sinking the Runciman managed *Empire Hawksbill* with the loss of all 46 crew and gunners, and damaging *Lavington Court* which was taken in tow for the U.K. and made 700 miles progress but sank when 300 miles west of Valencia. *Wellington* had taken on board the crew of *Lavington Court* soon after that ship was torpedoed and with the cutter *Gorleston* attacked the U-Boat that same afternoon without result. The convoy had meanwhile been diverted to the SE to avoid the U-Boats while an escorting aircraft helped to keep them submerged. The convoy and escorts reached Freetown on the 30th.

On 4 August, *Wellington, Folkestone, Gorleston*, corvette *Penstemon* and ex Bibby AMC *Cheshire* left Freetown as escort to convoy SL 118 of 34 ships. This was the last Freetown convoy to have an AMC as part of the escort, most of this type having been converted for trooping or upgraded to patrol independently in the South Atlantic or Indian Oceans. All went well with this convoy until the evening of the 17th when it reached a position 150 miles NE of the Azores where it was being shadowed by no less than four U-Boats. A successful attack was made by *U 566* which sank the Wilhelmsen *Triton* carrying a valuable cargo of wool and wheat from Australia. *Wellington* and *Penstemon* searched for this U-Boat without success, and 24 hours later *U 214* fired a spread of four torpedoes which not only sank the Dutch *Balingkar* and B.I. *Hatarana* but also seriously damaged the AMC *Cheshire,* although she was able to continue with the convoy. A further 24 hours later, *U 406* sank the Ellerman *City of Manila* and by which time escorting aircraft deterred the U-Boats from further attack. The one redeeming feature of these sinkings was that only three lives were lost amongst the 339 crew on the four ships involved. No further attacks were made on this convoy which reached Liverpool on the 26[th,] *Wellington* having detached into 'Derry two days earlier.

After seven days in harbour and with one more trip to make in 1942 on the Freetown convoys *Wellington* sailed from 'Derry on 31 August and joined the escort of OS 39 of 28 ships. There were no losses on passage, the convoy reached Freetown on 18 September, having previously detached the long range escorts into Bathurst. The return passage began on the 23rd as escort to SL 123 of 27 ships, from which the sloop detached on 10 October and joined convoy XK 1 from Gibraltar, until detaching again into 'Derry on the 15th.

On reaching home waters it was found that a massive seaborne operation to land British and US forces in North Africa was about to be launched from the U.K., making such heavy demands on escorts that convoys to and from Freetown had to be suspended. This remained in force for five months, during which time shipping en route to the South Atlantic was diverted via the North Atlantic and eastern seaboard of the U.S.

CHAPTER 8

LONDONDERRY 42nd ESCORT GROUP

Wellington had an extended period in 'Derry of 32 days, when additional 20mm guns were mounted to assist in air defence, while Lieut. L G Toone, RN was appointed as the new Commanding Officer; the gradual reduction in rank of the most recent COs matching the reduced status of the ship in the newly formed 42nd Escort Group, to operate with the fast troop convoys to North Africa. This Group comprised the sloops *Weston* (Commander L F Durnford Slater, RN, Senior Officer 42nd EG), *Folkestone*, *Wellington*, cutters *Gorleston* and *Totland,* new River class frigate *Waveney* and corvette *Azalea*. *Wellington* was rated 5th in seniority within the Group.

The ships of 42nd Escort Group sailed from 'Derry on 13 November and assembled at the Tail of the Bank off Greenock later that day. All Commanding Officers attended the convoy conference next morning with the Masters of the 15 troopships sailing from the Clyde, which included two P&O *Straths*, two Orient liners and two from Canadian Pacific. The main Torch convoy carrying British and US troops for the landings at Algiers and Oran had sailed on 26 October with a follow-up convoy five days later; subsequent sailings with reinforcements thereafter sailed at fortnightly intervals.

KMF 3 was the first of the 'build-up' convoys and sailed from the Clyde with 42 EG at 1600 on 14 November. At 0130 next morning to the South of Islay, *Wellington* investigated a suspicious Radar contact which proved to be aeroplane wreckage, of which only the twin tailplane, similar to a Lockheed Lightning remained visible. Three further troopships including Royal Mail's *Andes*, joined from Liverpool just before 0800 in a position 20 miles NW of Tory Island, from which point the convoy was routed to the SW as interference from enemy aircraft in UK waters had virtually ceased.

The KMF convoys and their returning MKF counterparts were provided with shore-based daylight air escort throughout most of their passage while the Escort Groups were able to give a more complete A/S screen than that afforded the Freetown convoys. Some of the liners of KMF 3 could attain 22 knots, but the slowest ships determined the convoy maximum of 14.5 knots, less an allowance for zigzag to give an average over the ground of 13 to 14 knots. The convoy was disposed in three columns with the Commodore

(RNR) embarked on *Strathallan*. The total number of troops embarked on the 18 transports (three being American) was almost 60,000.

There were a number of minor incidents on passage. *Wellington*'s Asdic was out of action for an hour on the 16th. *Waveney* obtained a doubtful contact next day and dropped two charges but was thought to be fish. *Azalea* was unable to keep station on the 17th due to stress of weather and was ordered independently to the next position. *Waveney* had a breakdown of steering gear on the 18th but repaired this in just over an hour. Next day the Radar on *Weston* developed a fault when *Folkestone* assumed general guard. Also on that date *Gorleston*, which was acting as HF/DF guard, reported interceptions which indicated an attack being planned by a U-Boat 30 miles ahead but nothing developed. At 0700 on the 20th the convoy was 75 miles SW of Cape St. Vincent and two hours later was met by Captain D3 in the destroyer *Milne* with *Quiberon*, *Quality* and *Quentin* which formed an advance screen four miles ahead. Doubtful contacts were obtained and charges dropped that same day while *Gorleston*'s Radar developed a defect but was rectified by a spare condenser transferred from *Wellington*. The Hunt class destroyer *Avon Vale* joined that evening as additional A/S escort.

The convoy passed through the Straits of Gibraltar late on the 20th, five liners detached with the D3 destroyers for Oran next afternoon while the remaining ships with 42 EG arrived outside Algiers at 0900 on the 22nd, some anchoring in the Bay and others with military stores for discharge berthing within the harbour.

The Commodore of KMF 3 reported that the convoy experienced moderate to fine weather with no incidents of importance, but the SOE on *Weston* revealed 'the escorts were continually hampered by their small excess of speed' and with 'the convoy steaming at 14.5 knots, the slower escorts were at full speed continuously' to keep up. 'Any offensive action' would have meant them being absent 'on the screen for many hours... .The question of rescuing survivors... in the event of a torpedoing... caused me considerable anxiety'. [15]

After eight days and nights hard steaming, the crews of 42 EG were doubtless looking forward to a run ashore amongst the delights of Algiers but were quickly disillusioned. All ships had to be rapidly fuelled and watered while the troops and stores disembarked or transferred to smaller ships for onward passage to Bone. During the nights of 22 and 23 November the port was subjected to heavy air attacks when the Cunard *Scythia*, at anchor, was struck forward by an aerial torpedo but survived to berth in the harbour next day, and after repairs there and at Oran, Gibraltar and New York was out of service for seven months.

Six of the liners were emptied and cleared the port in the afternoon of the 23rd for Gibraltar, while four others sailed 24 hours later to be joined by the five from Oran, leaving *Scythia* and two others behind. The complete convoy re-assembled at Gibraltar on being joined by another Orient liner and the escort carrier *Archer* to make convoy MKF 3 of 17 ships still under escort of 42 EG less *Azalea*, plus two of the ex US Town class destroyers as additional A/S escort to help prevent the losses which had occurred with two earlier MKF formations.

Convoy MKF 3 sailed from Gibraltar on the afternoon of 26 November with the same Commodore on *Strathallan* and formed into six columns with *Wellington* and *Weston* stationed 45°, 2 miles on the port and starboard bows respectively. The carrier *Archer* flew off A/S air patrols as and when the weather allowed, *Folkestone* was unable to maintain station on the afternoon of the 27th due to weather which caused a reduction in the convoy speed, and that same afternoon when 100 miles west of St. Vincent, two Spanish trawlers from Vigo were encountered, both were fitted with W/T and were closed by *Gorleston* and ordered not to report the convoy by that or any other means.

The convoy had passed 35 miles south of St. Vincent and by the 30th was 450 miles west of Ushant when indications of U-Boats ahead caused the Admiralty to order an alteration of course and *Archer* to maintain continuous air patrols until dusk. A Sunderland was also present that forenoon but no enemy interference occurred. *Lancaster* was detached that evening to Milford Haven due to shortage of fuel.

By daylight 1 December the convoy was 130 miles west of Valentia, and four hours later detached two US transports to proceed independently to New York, sadly one was torpedoed and sunk en route with the loss of all her crew and armed guard on board. Four columns were formed that afternoon followed by two columns next morning as the convoy neared Inishtrahull, passing 5 miles off at 0745 and at 0830 detaching five of the escorts including *Wellington* into Lough Foyle to fuel. Four of the liners were then detached for Liverpool while the remaining ten arrived in the Clyde at 1500 that same day. The SOE in his report drew attention to the most valuable addition of the two Town class destroyers to the escort; the Commodore made little comment on the passage but asked that liners with cargo for Algiers should have it distributed amongst three or four hatches to speed up discharge and so allow all ships to be cleared from the port within a single day.

After eight days in harbour, *Wellington* left 'Derry with 42 EG on 10 December, proceeding to the Clyde to attend the convoy conference for KMF 5. The convoy Commodore, as with KMF 3, was another officer of the RNR who was also accommodated with his staff on *Strathallan* (Master -Captain JH Biggs) which was embarked with 4,632 troops. Three other transports and a storeship comprised the Clyde section of the convoy which sailed at 0300 on the 12th with the ferry carrier *Argus*, destroyer *Laforey* and 42 EG comprising *Weston* (SO), *Folkestone*, *Gorleston*, *Wellington*, *Totland* and *Waveney*. Three more transports and three US storeships from Liverpool joined in the North Channel at midday.

The passage of KMF 5 was dominated for the first five days by a succession of SW'ly gales, causing the convoy to reduce speed at times to 8 kts. to ensure the A/S screen remained on station. One of the American storeships straggled on the first night out and did not rejoin; during the next night *Wellington* suffered some weather damage (unspecified) and had to put back to 'Derry, arriving there on the 15th. The three remaining storeships lost the convoy between 13 and 16 December and proceeded independently to Gibraltar; *Strathallan* was torpedoed to the north of Oran on the 21st and sank under tow, incredibly only six lives were lost out of the reported 5,445 persons on board.

Whatever the damage to *Wellington*, eight days were spent in 'Derry making this good, whereupon she sailed again two days before Christmas to execute the latter part of her previous orders, i.e. rejoining 42 EG as escort to the homeward MKF 5. The sloop proceeded south at 13 kts. and joined the convoy at 1730 on the 27th in a position 270 miles west of The Burlings. The carrier *Argus* was also with this convoy which comprised eight empty transports with the KMF 5 Commodore now on *Dunnottar Castle*. The homeward passage proved uneventful, no enemy being sighted and the convoy was off Tory Island on the morning of the 31st and arrived in the Clyde late that afternoon. The zigzag speed of 13.5 kts. was maintained by allowing the slowest ship, *Orduna* of 12.8 kts. to proceed on a straight course. The escorts arrived in 'Derry for a welcome New Year break of nine days, having been at sea in fast convoys for 75 percent of the past seven weeks.

'Derry had then become the principal escort base in the UK with 13 groups based in the port which included 20 destroyers, 14 sloops, 47 corvettes and 7 cutters, a total of 88 vessels in comparison to 58 in Liverpool. By January 1945 the 'Derry strength reached 131 vessels and by which time five fuelling berths were built close within the entrance to the river Foyle at Lisahally. In 'Derry itself there was 7,000 feet of quayage with depths up to 24 feet and sufficient width for escorts to turn in the river. The value of this base only just outwith neutral Eire yet giving the quickest access to the Western Approaches was quite immense.

While continuing as Senior Officer of 42 EG, *Weston* sailed alone to the Clyde and left there with troop convoy KMF 7 at 2300 on 8 January 1943 comprising three British transports, two Polish, one Belgian and one Norwegian all bound for North Africa. The Commodore, Vice Admiral BC Watson, RN, was embarked on *Monarch of Bermuda* (Captain WA Charlton). At 0930 off Orsay next morning, two other transports joined from Liverpool while *Folkestone, Totland, Wellington, Gorleston* and *Wear* formed the A/S screen with *Weston*. Also in the convoy was the Fleet Repair Ship *Wayland* (ex Cunard *Antonia)* bound for Gibraltar, the two slowest ships *Orbita* and *Leopoldville* both 14.5 kts. dictated the speed of advance which averaged 12.47 kts. for the voyage.

Heavy weather was encountered on passage to Gibraltar but no enemy interference developed. Just before midday on the 13th, the Canadian Pacific *Duchess of Bedford* caught up and joined, having been delayed leaving Liverpool; this was in a position 350 miles west of Lisbon. The convoy passed through the Gibraltar straits in the evening of the 15th, where *Wayland* was detached, and next afternoon two of the transports detached into Oran where also an American tanker joined. Algiers was safely reached next morning.

The returning convoy MKF 7 comprised the same eight now empty transports, and with six storeships, left Algiers with 42 EG at 1800 on the 18th, with Commodore Watson continuing on *Monarch of Bermuda.* At 1100 next day, the other two transports rejoined from Oran with another storeship while one of the latter was detached. At 0800 on the 20th, five storeships were detached into Gibraltar with three of the transports which were then continuing to West Africa. Also at this point two further transports joined, one being the French *Ville d'Oran* which was requisitioned for MOWT charter in Algiers as a troopship and subsequently placed under Cunard management. As with the outward convoy, MKF 7 enjoyed flat calm conditions in the Mediterranean and moderately heavy weather in the Atlantic. The convoy had an uneventful passage and entered the North Channel on the 25th, where three of the transports were detached for Liverpool while the escorts detached into 'Derry to leave the Clyde-bound ships in charge of a local escort for that port. In concluding his report of the voyage, the Commodore commented on the admirable behaviour of the escorts throughout the voyage 'and the fact that they maintained their positions... with frequent heavy weather in proceeding at nearly their maximum speed was highly creditable to all concerned'.[15]

Wellington was now due for annual refit and after three days in 'Derry sailed for Sheerness where she arrived on 1 February for a period of almost ten weeks, during which time it is believed that 4×20mm Oerlikon guns and the Hedgehog ahead throwing A/S weapon were fitted, while the 3 inch HA gun was removed. The steadily increasing armament, radar and HF/DF also meant additional personnel, bringing the ship's complement up to 11 officers and 120 ratings, i.e. 22 per cent more than in peacetime and therefore made for cramped conditions, but equalled by all escorts at that time. The status of the ship was also somewhat restored at this time when Commander J T Jones, RD RNR was appointed to command on 4 March. After re-commissioning with a Chatham crew, the sloop departed Sheerness on 10 April and returned to 'Derry three days later to rejoin 42 Escort Group for further service with the KMF convoys.

By February 1943 it became necessary for the Admiralty to re-start the outward OS and homeward SL convoys to and from Freetown, which were suspended by the shortage of escorts occasioned by the Torch convoys and subsequent two weekly cycle of the KMF series to North Africa. There was in addition the need to continue the monthly flow of reinforcements and supplies to Eighth Army in the Middle East and Fourteenth Army in Burma, served by the WS convoys passing round the Cape to Suez and Bombay. The continuing shortage of escorts meant that all these demands could only be met by combining the departure of WS convoys with every second KMF convoy and to sail them as a single convoy until splitting to the west of Gibraltar whence the WS portion continued towards the Cape while the KMF section proceeded to Oran and Algiers. This system began with the departure of WS 26 and KMF 8 in January 1943.

The combined convoy of WS 29/KMF 13 comprised 17 transports embarked with almost 49,000 troops, plus 7 storeships, and sailed in three separate sections from the Bristol Channel, Liverpool and the Clyde to a rendezvous off Orsay at 1600 on 16 April, where also 42 EG formed the A/S screen. The group left 'Derry that morning and held an escort conference off Moville at 0930 before proceeding on exercises en route to the rendezvous. The group now comprised the sloops *Weston* and *Wellington*, frigates *Exe* and *Ness*, cutters *Gorleston* and *Totland* while three destroyers and the cruiser *Newcastle* were assigned to the WS section. A speed of 12.25 knots was set on the initial course out to the westward until 0700 next day when an alteration was made to SW and 24 hours later to South to pass 250 miles west of Finisterre.

The cruiser *Charybdis* joined at 1500 on the 18th on the latitude of the Scillies to provide additional AA protection against enemy interference but none was encountered. Shortly after midday 19th an Admiralty message stated an enemy aircraft had reported a convoy which may have been WS 29/KMF 13 but no avoiding action was taken as the formation was due to make a wide alteration that evening and reckoned to be a sufficient diversion from the original line of advance.

By the afternoon of the 20th the convoy was 140 miles west of Lisbon and that evening one of the liners was detached independently for New York. *Charybdis* detached soon after as the convoy was now out of range of the Focke-Wulf Condors based at Bordeaux. At daybreak 21st course was altered to ESE towards the Straits of Gibraltar and at 1000 the split position was reached, 30 miles south of St. Vincent, where the WS 29 section detached nine points to starboard with destroyer escort towards Cape Ghir and Freetown. The eleven liners and 42 EG of KMF 13 continued towards the Straits and arrived at Algiers at 0845 on the 23rd after detaching one liner into Gibraltar and two others for Oran.

After the (by now) usual day and a half in Algiers, the return convoy MKF 13 sailed at 1930 on 24 April of eight liners with 42 EG, and next morning were joined by the two previously left at Oran. When passing Gibraltar at 0230 on the 26th, two transports were detached for that port while six others joined up, almost colliding with the convoy by approaching at right angles from the starboard beam, although the night was clear with the moon up. The convoy then set off on the route laid down towards the U.K.

There were no reported incidents until the evening of the 29th when in the approach to home waters and on the latitude of Ushant. The convoy was steaming at 14.5 kts. in five columns and zigzagging, when a Focke-Wulf Condor aircraft was sighted on the port beam and soon joined by another. Both 'circled the convoy at a very low altitude for half an hour, opening the range when fired upon by the nearest escorts. Subsequently three high level bombing attacks were made by one aircraft at a time and at a height of about 10,000 feet'.[15] In the first attack two 500 lb. bombs exploded about 200 yards from the US transport *Argentina*. There were no bombs in the second attack while in the third the aircraft had to evade the accurate shooting of *Argentina* although two bombs fell between two of the Dutch flag transports. After dark the convoy altered course to NE for four hours. No further attacks were made and on reaching the North Channel in the evening of 1 May, the convoy dispersed to proceed independently to destination: *Wellington* and 42 EG proceeding to Greenock where they arrived on the morning of the 2nd to remain for 17 days.

During the process of preparing the next combined WS/KMF convoy from the U.K., all Axis resistance ceased in Tunisia to end three years of warfare in North Africa. This paved the way for the next phase of landing in Sicily and reopening the Mediterranean for through traffic three months later. The WS convoys were now on a very much reduced scale with less than 11,000 embarking on a mere five transports of WS 30, of which four were American. Two cargo liners were also accompanying the convoy for the first few days.

The composition of KMF 15 was eleven transports and two small commissioned LSIs being returned to the Mediterranean after refits. Troops were embarked in Liverpool and on the Clyde but all five transports of WS 30 and eight of these in KMF 15 sailed from the Clyde at 1800 on 19 May, to rendezvous with the remaining three from Liverpool at 0530 next day off Orsay. The combined escort was provided by the cruiser *Suffolk*, AMC *Corfu*, ferry carrier *Unicorn* ferrying Beaufighter aircraft to Gibraltar, three destroyers also for Gibraltar and 42 Escort Group now strengthened by the sloop *Lowestoft* to seven units and going all the way to Algiers.

Off Orsay the convoy formed into seven columns, the WS section conveniently being the three starboard columns for ease of detachment at the split position. The usual W'ly course was at first followed, then SW and SSW to a position 400 miles west of Ushant on the 22nd, then South for the next two days and passing 300 miles west of Finisterre on the 23rd. Some of the escort dropped charges on the 21st and 22nd without results, and again on the 24th as the convoy steered SE towards the split position. That afternoon a Focke-Wulf was seen on and off for an hour and a half, presumably spotting for U-Boats. Some ships fired off a few rounds at extreme range while

Unicorn was favoured with a few near misses and flew off a "Seafire" to intercept but sadly this aircraft was unable to make contact._

The split position, 90 miles south of Cape St. Vincent was reached on the forenoon of the 25th, where KMF 15 of eleven transports, the two LSIs, *Unicorn*, three destroyers and 42 EG detached towards the Straits leaving WS 30 with *Suffolk* to continue towards Freetown and the Cape. *Unicorn* with the destroyers and one transport detached into Gibraltar, two other transports into Oran while the remaining eight with 42 EG reached Algiers on the 27th.

The return convoy MKF 15 with the same eight transports and 42 EG set out from Algiers at 1830 on 28 May. Outside Oran at 1030 next day they were joined by three British and four US transports, the latter group embarked with German POW for the U.K., and three US storeships. Arriving off Europa Point at 0430 on the 30th, the storeships were detached into Gibraltar as were three British transports being sent on to West Africa. In replacement eight other transports joined from Gibraltar, the damaged *Scythia* (from KMF 3) en route to New York, one US transport from Casablanca for the U.K. and six British transports homeward bound from the Cape and beyond, which had been routed through Gibraltar to join the safety of an MKF convoy.

The completed convoy now of 20 transports in five columns of four, departed the Straits with Commodore D A Casey, RNR remaining on the Cunard *Samaria* (Captain H R Oulsram) from the outward trip. The 42 EG was now strengthened by two fleet destroyers with the escort carrier *Tracker* and repair carrier *Unicorn*. When 80 miles west of the Straits *Totland* was detached back to Gibraltar and at 0130 on 1 June when 280 miles west of The Burlings, *Scythia* was detached independently for New York and where she arrived eight days later for damage repairs in drydock.

By the evening of 1 June the convoy was 300 miles west of Finisterre where an enemy aircraft dropped four bombs off the starboard bow of the Dutch transport *Indrapoera* but without causing major damage. There were no further incidents on passage; MKF 15 arrived safely in the North Channel in the afternoon of 4 June and was dispersed, with 14 transports continuing to the Clyde and the remaining five to Liverpool. *Wellington* and 42 EG berthed in 'Derry that same day.

This was to become the last visit of *Wellington* to 'Derry which had served as her home port for almost two years. The escort strength of the RN had grown from 33 sloops in September 1939 to 341 units of six types by the end of June 1943 and was to double again within the next two years. With faster and better armed frigates and destroyer escorts coming into service, the ships of 42 Escort Group were to be dispersed for less onerous tasks than high speed troop convoys, *Wellington* being assigned to West Africa. Command of the ship now devolved on Commander G A Thring, DSO RN, effective on 18 June.

Wellington left 'Derry on 19 June to become the principal escort of the first convoy to leave the U.K. for the assault landings on Sicily, designated KMS 18A and comprising eight LST, one LSG and a small Petrol Carrier. This convoy sailed from the Clyde on the 20th and five days later reached a position 250 miles NW of Finisterre, having averaged 8.5 kts. but was then reduced to 6.5 kts. and subsequently arrived at Gibraltar on the 29th to await the arrival of the storeships following behind as KMS 18B. The *Wellington* group left Gibraltar on 3 July and joined with the storeship convoy north of Algiers on the 5th, from which the sloop detached as ordered to return westward and join the escort of a small convoy RS 8 en route from Gibraltar to Freetown. The sloop detached from this convoy to refuel at Casablanca on the 7th but resumed escort and reached Freetown seven days later and was there assigned to West Africa Command.

CHAPTER 9

WEST AFRICA COMMAND

In May 1943 six U-Boats arrived off Freetown to repeat earlier successes and at first sank 12 ships by the end of that month; thereafter they sank only one ship in each of the next three months and by January 1944 had entirely left the area. The task of *Wellington* with three other sloops and 15 corvettes, split into three groups, was to provide escort to the many coastal convoys moving between Freetown in Sierra Leone, Takoradi on the Gold Coast and Lagos in Nigeria. The distance between the first two ports was 800 miles and a further 320 miles to Lagos. Passage time eastbound from Freetown gained by the favourable Guinea current which could attain 3 knots in the summer months but less so in winter when the easterly Harmattan winds can reduce its strength. Even so these were slow convoys taking three or four days to Takoradi eastbound but five or six days in the opposite direction. The constant heat and high humidity, especially in Freetown where it frequently reached 90 per cent, was a drain on the constitution of the escort crews living and working aboard very hot ships.

During the nine months spent on the West African coast, *Wellington* escorted seven convoys in each direction, mostly direct to Lagos but others calling at Takoradi en route. There was little recreation available in Takoradi but the time spent in Lagos which varied from two to 14 days was the high spot on the coast, where parties were laid on with nurses from an Army General Hospital and WAAFs stationed at the air transit base. Port time in Freetown varied from a single day to 18 days. There was one recorded interruption by the enemy on 18 August when the sloop was escorting a local westbound convoy form Lagos to Takoradi. The sloop attacked this U-Boat with depth charges and claimed a kill which was initially disputed by the Admiralty but re-assessed six months later as 'probably sunk'. The author has been unable to substantiate this claim from post war records.

Wellington was at sea with a convoy between Freetown and Lagos on Christmas Day 1943 and left Lagos for the return passage on New Year's Eve. Some light relief from the coastal trips was provided on 22 January when the sloop left Freetown with the homeward convoy SL 147 of 28 ships, but was to remain only for the first three days until relieved by the Bathurst based escorts when detached and returned to Freetown.

Three more round trip convoys were escorted to and from Lagos up until arrival Freetown on 18 April 1944, by which time the sloop became due for annual refit and as no facilities were available on the West African coast, arrangements were made for this work to be undertaken at the Admiralty dockyard in Bermuda.

The sloop left Freetown on 22 April as escort to the homeward convoy SL 156 of 23 ships and continued with this formation until 2 May, when to the SW of Cape St. Vincent, detachment was made direct for Bermuda which was reached six days later. The Bermuda refit lasting 12 weeks in a pleasant climate with excellent shoreside facilities must have been a welcome respite from the rigours of West Africa. During this time Temp. Acting Lieut. Commander C A Shilllan, RNVR assumed command, effective on 22 May and remained for a period of five months.

The long awaited D Day assault on Europe took place while the sloop was in Bermuda and by the date of her departure on 29 July, US forces were breaking out of the Normandy bridgehead. *Wellington* was directed first to St. John's, Newfoundland where she arrived on 2 August and left three days later on a direct seven day passage to the Clyde, where three weeks were spent, possibly making good defects from the recent refit. It was during this period that Acting Lieut. Commander A Hague RD RNR became the ship's final Commanding officer with effect from 21 August. He was later to become a long standing Member of The Honourable Company of Master Mariners, and survived to join the Duke of Edinburgh at a special Members' Luncheon held on board in December 1998, to celebrate the 50th anniversary of *Wellington* arriving at Victoria Embankment in London.

Wellington departed the Clyde on 2 September, exercised and briefly worked up en route to fuelling at Belfast on the 4th before joining the escort of convoy OS 88 of 28 ships bound to Freetown. This convoy was attached to KMS 62 of 16 ships until the split position was reached to the west of Gibraltar on the 10th, the sloop then continuing south with OS 88, refuelling en route in Casablanca and reaching Freetown on the 21st. Three days were spent there before the sloop reverted to a brief series of coastal convoys to and from Lagos and Takoradi, until arrival Freetown on 16 December where she was assigned to 55 Escort Group of the Mediterranean Fleet, and immediately after Boxing Day was given the task of escorting AFD 24 being towed by three of Smit's Dutch flag tugs from Freetown to Gibraltar.

The tow left Freetown on 30 December and made a good passage of nine days to Gibraltar at an average speed of 9.25 kts. The next four weeks were spent refitting in Gibraltar, the ship now beginning to show her age of eleven years since completion but more significantly approaching six years of hard service as a convoy escort, and now totally eclipsed by the rapidly increasing fleet of heavily armed 20 knot frigates and destroyer escorts, of which no less than 275 were already in service on the Home Commands.

CHAPTER 10

55ᵗʰ ESCORT GROUP BASED ON GIBRALTAR

The war in Europe and on the Atlantic was to last a mere three months by the time *Wellington* completed the Gibraltar refit on 4 February 1945, on which date she sailed as escort to the homeward convoy MKS 81 of 28 ships, continuing only for the first two days when detached to join the outbound KMS 82 of 20 ships which brought her back to Gibraltar on the 9ᵗʰ. Five days were spent in port before the sloop left with the corvettes *Willowherb* and *Spiraea* as EG 11 for a small convoy to Casablanca, returning to Gibraltar with another formation on the 18ᵗʰ. Two days later the sloop was sent to the westward to join the escort of KMS 95 and arrived back in port with this convoy on the 25ᵗʰ. Nine days were then given in harbour, during which time the sloop was ordered to form EG 3 with corvettes *Bergamot* and *Spiraea*, but left on 6 March with *Willowherb* as escort to MKS 87, continued for three days then switched to KMS 88 and arrived back in Gibraltar on the 11ᵗʰ. Three further MKS and KMS convoys were similarly covered in the next four weeks to 11 April, and on the 20ᵗʰ *Wellington* sailed westward for three days with MKS 96 of 27 ships and returned to port on the 24ᵗʰ.

By this date Russian forces had penetrated Berlin while British forces were attacking Bremen and clearly the war in Europe was drawing to a close but there was no slackening of the U-Boat war on the Atlantic. *Wellington* left Gibraltar on 27 April to rendezvous with the neutral Spanish steamer *Monte Monjuich* and accompanied her into Gibraltar two days later, and on the afternoon of 4 May Germany agreed the terms of surrender to become effective next day. All U-Boats were instructed to cease hostilities and return to base, but of 57 known to be in the Atlantic or in British inshore waters, only eight obeyed. On 8 May an Admiralty message advised that all U-Boats were instructed to surface and proceed to designated ports, but it was another week before this order was complied with to leave the seas once again free of that hated menace.

It was perhaps appropriate that *Wellington* sailed from Gibraltar on 5 May as the surrender became effective, escorting MKS 99 for the first three days of its homeward passage, before transferring to the outward KMS

A weather-worn *Wellington* entering Gibraltar,
15 April 1945

100, only to detach from this final convoy on the 9th when it was known that the first group of U-Boats had actually surrendered. *Wellington* and the 1935 built sloop *Enchantress* were then ordered to investigate U-Boats on passage to surrender in Gibraltar and on the 12th, the first named had the pleasure of receiving that acceptance from *U 541* which was escorted into Gibraltar that same day. This was a U-Boat on her fourth patrol which in two years service had only sunk one small ship, but nevertheless made an appropriate ending to almost six years continuous war service of *Wellington*.

There would be much relief and celebration amongst the warships berthed in Gibraltar at this time, with many ship's companies wondering if they were now to be turned eastward to join the Pacific Fleet in the war against Japan, but *Wellington*, indeed all the pre-war sloops were now hopelessly outclassed in both speed and armament and unlikely to be retained anywhere other than the Reserve Fleet.

One last task was now given to *Wellington* which left Gibraltar on the 21st and proceeded to a position 500 miles westward for Air Sea Rescue duties, until relieved by *Enchantress* on the 29th when she returned to port on the 31st. After eleven final days in Gibraltar, *Wellington* sailed for home on 11 June with the destroyer *Malcolm* and other escorts, but was diverted by the Admiralty en route to locate the Isles class trawler *Prospect* and did not reach Devonport until the 17th. Here the ship was prepared to go into reserve and sailed on 11 July for Liverpool, where de-storing took place over a period of 25 days.

The final passage of *Wellington* as an HM Ship was made from Liverpool to Pembroke Dock on 6 August 1945, where the ship paid off to the Reserve Fleet and was formally accepted there on the 19th of that month by being driven on to a mud berth at full speed with the anchors down, alongside other escorts now deemed redundant. The ship had steamed 66,367 miles in four years of peace and 248,586 miles in almost six years of war service, by providing escort either alone or in part to 103 convoys.

Eighteen months later the ship was sold to The Honourable Company of Master Mariners and on 6 February 1947 passed out of Admiralty control and records.

HMS WELLINGTON 1933–1947

HMS WELLINGTON COMMANDING OFFICERS

COMMANDING OFFICER	APPOINTED
Commander J B E Hall, RN	22/01/1935
Commander G N Loriston-Clarke, RN	21/11/1936
Commander R E Hyde-Smith, RN	07/01/1939
Commander I H Bockett-Pugh, DSO*, RN	26/10/1940
Lieut. Commander W F R Segrave, DSC*, RN	04/04/1941
Lieutenant L G Toone, RN	24/10/1942
Commander J T Jones, RD, RNR	04/03/1943
Commander G A Thring, DSO*, RN	18/06/1943
Temp. Act. Lieut. Commander C A Shillan, RNVR	22/05/1944
Act. Lieut. Commander A Hague, RD RNR	21/08/1944

* These decorations were gained while serving in other ships.

HMS WELLINGTON SUMMARY OF SERVICE

ITEM	DATES	PERIOD		
Under construction to trials	25/09/33–04/02/35	1 yr	4 m	10d
On passage to New Zealand station	04/02/35–20/05/35		3 m	14d
New Zealand station	20/05/35–03/09/39	4 yr	3 m	15d
On passage to East Indies station	03/09/39–19/09/39			16d
East Indies station	19/09/39–02/11/39		1m	4d
On passage to United Kingdom via West Africa	02/11/39–05/01/40		2m	3d
Unallocated–Cardiff Refit	05/01/40–29/01/40			24d
Western Approaches 1st Escort Division	29/01/40–07/07/40		5m	8d
Western Approaches Liverpool Division	07/07/40–27/08/41	1 yr	1m	21d
Western Approaches Londonderry Sloop Division	27/08/41–14/10/42	1 yr	1m	17d
Western Approaches Londonderry 42 Escort Group	14/10/42–14/07/43		8m	29d
West Africa Command	14/07/43–08/01/45	1 yr	5m	25d
Mediterranean Fleet, 55 Escort Group	08/01/45–06/08/45		6m	27d
Reserve Fleet, Milford Haven	06/08/45–06/02/47	1 yr	6m	01d
TOTAL ROYAL NAVY SERVICE		**13 yr**	**4m**	**12d**

REFIT PERIODS–VESSEL OUT OF SERVICE

ITEM	DATES	PERIOD
Auckland	29/04/36–17/06/36	49d
Auckland	27/01/37–15/03/37	47d
Sydney	03/05/38–13/06/38	41d
Sydney	24/02/39–31/03/39	35d
Cardiff	09/01/40–29/01/40	19d
Dundee	02/02/41–19/03/41	45d
Belfast	02/03/42–26/04/42	55d
Sheerness	01/02/43–10/04/43	68d
Bermuda	08/05/44–29/07/44	82d

THE COUNTER ATTACK: A/S SUMMARY FOR
=====================================
THE OFFICER OF THE WATCH.
========================

Attention is drawn to C.B. 4097-I-paras.
150 - 172.
=====================================

GENERAL.

1. A COUNTER ATTACK is to be carried out on any A/S contact obtained on the close screen of a convoy and, unless it is classified as "non-sub" during the run-in, a full 10 charge pattern should be fired.

2. The object of a Counter Attack is to harass a U-Boat which may be about to fire torpedoes at the convoy. The attack is carried out as quickly as possible, and the risk of own ship being "Gnatted" is accepted.

ACCURACY is sacrificed to SPEED.

ON OBTAINING A CONTACT ON THE CLOSE SCREEN.

    1.   Steer for the bearing of the contact.

    2.   Set revolutions for 14 knots.

    3.   Close up the D/C crew (shorts on the 4.7" cease-fire bell).

    4.   Set pattern E for 'Easy'.

    5.   Switch on No 2 recorder.

These five things are done without waiting for classification of the contact.

THE RUN-IN.

1. Operator: will give left and right out-ons of the target, Doppler and, if possible, movement of target

2. O.O.W.: a) Conn the ship: will deduct centre bearings from the operator's cut-ons and steer the ship at them; otherwise, true movement of the target cannot be found. If the movement is given, throw off in the direction of the movement, when the range is about 800 yards. If none is given, steer for the centre-bearings.

       b) Work the recorder: this will give range of target, Relative Speed of Approach and the time to fire.

FIRING DRILL.

1. Using the look-out as communications number when the range is 400 yards:

    a) Make the Bridge Selector Switch to "Depth Charge".

    b) Order "Stand-by" to the Afterguard by phone.

    c) Give one long push on the WARNING BUZZER: (this also warns the Engine Room).

2. Line up the Perspex firing bar with the recorder trace and when the left hand edge of the last inch of the trace comes under the dots on the firing bar, order "FIRE" and get the look-out to press the FIRING CLOCK starter-push.

NOTES.

1. SINGLE CHARGE: To fire a charge from the starboard rails set to 150 feet can be useful. It will put a U-Boat off its aim or disperse any fish and assist subsequent classification.

2. RECORDER SETTING: 14 knots and 200 feet (Pattern E) is always set.

3. TRANSMISSION RANGE: Keep the red pointer at 500 yards more than the range of the contact.

4. THROW-OFF: If you have made a good throw off, the bearing of the target will remain steady until the range is about 200 yards. It is better to throw off too much than too little.

5. WARNING THE CONVOY:

    By night: A burst of Oerlikon fire on the bearing.

    By day: Black pendant.

    a) At the dip: Am listening with special apparatus to some underwater object.

    b) Close up: Am listening with special apparatus to some underwater object and may drop depth charges.

6. CALLING THE CAPTAIN: A series of short rings on the Captain's bell.

[signature]

SUB. LIEUTENANT, R.N.V.R.
A/S CONTROL OFFICER

This reproduction, believed dated about August 1943 in the second half of the war, gives clear instructions to the Officer of the Watch of an Escort Vessel, for immediately attacking any Anti-Submarine contact found within the close screen of a convoy, without awaiting classification. Speed was seen as the essential element of attack.

CHAPTER 11

THE HONOURABLE COMPANY OF MASTER MARINERS
HQS WELLINGTON 1947–2005

Following the exceptional service rendered by the Mercantile Marine in the Great War of 1914–18, proposals emerged in 1921 which brought about the formation of 'The Company of Master Mariners' in 1926. This Company was incorporated by Royal Charter in 1930 and granted Livery by the Court of Aldermen at Guildhall in 1932, the first new Livery Company for over 200 years. At this same date suggestions were made for the purchase of one of the few remaining deepwater British sailing ships, for conversion into a Livery Hall and administration offices for the Company, berthed within the City, rather than continue in shore-based offices in Leadenhall Street.

There was also a scheme dating from 1929 to purchase a redundant tea warehouse on a most appropriate site on Tower Hill, overlooking the Pool of London, but this was not progressed and in 1943 the area was acquired for construction of the present day National Memorial to the Merchant Navy. As the 1930s progressed a further scheme emerged for all of the 'Hall-less' Livery Companies to pool their resources and erect a new building comprising separate offices but sharing a common hall. This plan remained in being up to the outbreak of the war in 1939, although the Master Mariners still preferred the floating hall project and actually made a bid for a suitable sailing ship in late August 1939 which had to be withdrawn when hostilities commenced.

With the return to peace in 1945 the old sailing ship was found to have deteriorated into a sorry state and also unsuitable for the berth previously arranged at Temple Stairs on the Embankment, under a privilege granted by the Benchers of Inner and Middle Temples. In March 1946 with the approach of the Company's 20th Anniversary the then Master urged a fresh look at the Hall question, and a month later it was suggested the Admiralty was prepared to offer the Company an escort of the *Grimsby* class at very advantageous terms, for conversion as a suitable HQ and which could be moored at Temple Stairs without difficulty.

There were 25 surviving sloops of the pre-war design declared surplus to requirements and being offered for sale. The first three were disposed of in 1946 and the remainder within six years, except *Fleetwood* which the Admiralty converted into a Radar Training Ship to serve them for another 12 years. Whether by chance or design, one of the Wardens and then Marine Superintendent of the Clan Line, was invited to join a party being taken to sea on *Fleetwood* for a demonstration of radar which was then hardly known aboard merchant ships. His impressions of radar are not recorded but he could not fail to have formed a view on the suitability of such a ship for conversion to a Livery Hall. The matter was certainly deliberated at great length, many believing a warship would not make a fitting home for Merchant Seamen, but in due course the advantages were seen to outweigh earlier misgivings and by January 1947 The Honourable Company accepted the Admiralty's offer to purchase HMS *Wellington* then lying on the mud adjacent to Pembroke Dock.

In February 1947 the ship was towed to Chatham Dockyard where the task of stripping and converting was to be undertaken. Specifications were drawn up and considerable progress made in the detail of moorings at the Embankment, which proved rather premature. It was initially hoped to have the ship ready for a resumption of the Annual Dinner on 25 June but both were impractical so the Press was entertained in the City on that date by the Founder, Sir Robert Burton-Chadwick, with the Deputy Master and Wardens, to make them aware of an appeal being launched for the conversion of the *Wellington* as the Company's headquarters. A 21st Anniversary Dinner was however held in the Mansion House in October.

By April 1948 the work at Chatham was progressing steadily. All the armaments, ship's boats, radar, searchlights, etc., together with main engines and boilers had been removed: the latter items being replaced by a Court Room and Lounge. On the Foc'sle Deck a Clerk's office and Committee Room were formed out of the Commanding Officer's accommodation, a Library and Smoke Room/Writing Room on the Upper Deck and Museum/Reception area on the Lower Deck. By October 1948 it was hoped to complete the work in November and on 9 December 1948 *Wellington* berthed at Temple Stairs on the Victoria Embankment.

The purchase price of the ship was met entirely by the membership while the public appeal, which finally raised £63,441 for the conversion and fitting out, was initially addressed to the Shipowners who contributed a massive 70% of the total. Others including many Shipbuilders (largely Clyde based), the Corporation of Lloyds, Lloyds Register, the London Underwriters Association, Trinity House (both London and Hull), the Carpenters Company and all manner of other organisations, individuals and members associated with ships and the sea helped to realise The Honourable Company's ambition of establishing their own Hall and offices within the City boundary, a mere 22 years after its formation. There were many gifts of kind from members and companies involved in the fitting out, ranging from tableware and Court Room chairs, to the oak panelling for that same room given by the shipbreakers at Dalmuir who demolished the Shaw Savill liner *Themistocles*, and the magnificent teak staircase over two decks, saved from the day passenger steamer *Snaefell* (ex *Viper*) being broken up at Port Glasgow and donated by Commander J C Munro, RNR (Rtd).

The ship and hall was soon established on the Livery calendar. The Annual Service at St Michaels, Cornhill in March 1949 was followed by the AGM held aboard in the Court Room. HRH The Duke of Edinburgh visited in May while the King and Queen attended and were photographed with members of the Court in October. The Company had come of age and celebrated with a Silver Jubilee Dinner in the Mansion House in June 1951.

By 1958 the ship had been ten years at Temple Stairs and a drydocking was arranged over a quiet fortnight in August at R & H Green & Silley Weir's facility in Blackwall. A second drydocking was made in August 1970 at the London Graving Dock within the South West India complex. This was a more extensive docking and by which time a general office was in being on the Upper Deck in lieu of the library which had moved to the forward end of the Reception Area one deck below. New piping and pumping systems were fitted at this docking, a ladies' cloakroom provided together with shipkeeper's rest and locker room. Dredging of the berth at Temple Stairs was carried out by the PLA during the ship's absence.

On 29 July 1991 the ship was moved to Sheerness drydock for an extensive refit by the Medway Drydock & Engineering Co. This involved much replating on the Foc'sle and Upper Decks, the extension of office space and provision of a fully fitted galley commensurate with the hire of the ship's facilities in procuring income to offset the expenditure on maintenance. During the ship's absence of 93 days, the Wardens, Court and Ladies' Night Dinner were held at Trinity House.

Arriving back from Sheerness refit, 30 October 1991

Much additional work and improvements have been made *in situ* since that drydocking, including air conditioning in the Court Room, further enhancement of offices, extension of members' cabins, the Court Room re-panelled with improved lighting, and a more suitable boarding arrangement at the main entrance.

Wellington was granted World Ship Trust status in 2004 and, in looking to her long-term preservation, a Charitable Trust was incorporated under the Companies Act in January 2005 and registered as a charity in April that year. The ship was appropriately transferred to **The Wellington Trust** on 1 July 2005.

ABBREVIATIONS

A/A	- Anti Aircraft
ADC	- Aide de Camp
AFD	- Admiralty Floating Dock
AMC	- Armed Merchant Cruiser (Passenger Liner conversion)
A/S	- Anti Submarine
BEF	- British Expeditionary Force
CinC	- Commander-in-Chief
CinCWA	- Commander-in-Chief, Western Approaches
CO	- Commanding Officer
CPO	- Chief Petty Officer
DG	- De-gaussing
ERA	- Engine-Room Artificer
H.E.	- His Excellency (i.e. the High Commissioner)
HF/DF	- High Frequency Direction Finding
Kts.	- Nautical Miles per hour
LSG	- Landing Ship Gantry (Converted RFA tankers)
LSI	- Landing Ship Infantry
LST	- Landing Ship Tank
MOWT	- Ministry of War Transport
NE	- North East, similarly NW, SW, SE.
PO	- Petty Officer
PRO	- Public Record Office
RFA	- Royal Fleet Auxilary
RIB	- Rigid Inflatable Boat
SOE	- Senior Officer Escort
VIP	- Very Important Person (such as the Commissioner for the Western Pacific when visiting remote islands)
W/T	- Wireless Telegraphy (e.g. Morse) or Watertight Door

NOTES TO THE TEXT

(1)   - Arnold Hague, *Sloops 1926–46,* World Ship Society 1993, p.11.

(2)   - Accommodation layout as per General Arrangement Drawings Devonport Yard Constructive Department 15 Feb. 1935.

(3)   - Nelson Evening Mail, 10 October 1935.

(4)   - New Zealand Herald, 21 May 1935.

(5)   - New Zealand Herald, 23 September 1935.

(6)   - Fiji Times, 11 September 1935.

(7)   - Nelson Evening Mail, 18 October 1935.

(8)   - The Southland Times, 14 February 1936.

(9)   - Pacific Islands Pilot, Vol, 3, 1935, p.83.

(10)   - New Zealand Herald, 29 January 1937.

(11)   - New Zealand Herald, 2 August 1937.

(12)   - New Zealand Herald, 1 February 1938.

(13)   - The Times, London, 4 January 2003.

(14)   - The Fiji Times, 9 August 1939.

(15)   - PRO, ADM 199/720 and 199/1216

(16)   - Pacific Islands Pilot, Vol 1, 6th edition 1936.

(17)   - Lieut. Commander BH de Mellor, First Lieutenant 1937–40.

LIST OF ILLUSTRATIONS